Crime School:
Money Laundering

Crime School: Money Laundering

Chris Mathers

KEY PORTER BOOKS

National Library of Canada Cataloguing in Publication

Mathers, Chris
  Crime school : money laundering / Chris Mathers.

Includes bibliographical references and index.
ISBN 1-55263-584-8

1. Money laundering. I. Title.

HV6768.M27 2004   364.16'8   C2004-900384-4

The publisher gratefully acknowledges the support of the Canada Council for the Arts and the Ontario Arts Council for its publishing program. We acknowledge the support of the Government of Ontario through the Ontario Media Development Corporation's Ontario Book Initiative.

We acknowledge the financial support of the Government of Canada through the Book Publishing Industry Development Program (BPIDP) for our publishing activities.

Key Porter Books Limited
70 The Esplanade
Toronto, Ontario
Canada M5E 1R2

www.keyporter.com

Text design: Peter Maher
Electronic formatting: Jean Lightfoot Peters

Printed and bound in Canada

04 05 06 07 08 09 5 4 3 2 1

This book is dedicated to three friends, who never got the chance to read it.

Rob Rebeyka
Jacques Houde
Vern Miller

"To live in hearts we leave behind
is not to die"

Thomas Campbell
(1777–1844)

CONTENTS

FOREWORD

Chris Mathers was an outstanding undercover police officer. That is my opinion, but I am sure it will be shared by the readers of this book.

A career in law enforcement is more than a career, it is a vocation, if not a divine call. The work is all-consuming, often to the exclusion and detriment of some of the other important things in life, such as home and family. Police officers belong to a brotherhood/sisterhood whose intricate customs and language transcend the corporate limits of individual police departments, and indeed international borders. One need only witness a meeting of two strangers who learn that they both are or were police officers to know that a commonality of values, experience and respect exists among law enforcement professionals, whatever their language or culture.

In the community of policing, those who choose to be undercover officers are different, some would say odd, but definitely in a class by themselves. Undercover officers share many similar traits: they do not look like police officers, they love to act, they thrive on the excitement of the "sting" and think quickly on their feet and "outside of the box," knowing that lives are on the line—often their own. As is the case in any line of endeavor, some undercover police officers are better than others. Chris Mathers was among the best.

Chris grew up in Montreal and speaks French and English fluently. He also speaks Spanish and Italian, and can get by in Cantonese. He is a human chameleon who can quickly take on the demeanor, attitudes and speech patterns of those around him. Chris is extremely well read and articulate. Among a group of engineers, someone will soon ask him where he acquired his degree in engineering. As readers of this book will discover, he also has a great sense of humor—which is, I think, a survival mechanism for those whose lives are at risk on a daily basis, those who see too much of the seedy side of life.

This is not just a book for police officers. Anyone who has ever been curious about the people who commit crimes, especially those who "launder" money, and the people who solve crimes will find it fascinating. In inimitable Mathers style, drawing on his own twenty years of experience as an undercover money launderer, he removes much of the mystery of the underworld inhabited by the "bad guys." He knows the special lingo the crooks use, and the many schemes and tricks they employ to deal with the difficult problem of having too much ill-gotten cash—cash that they want to slip undetected into the legitimate economy. He also demonstrates the strange fact that not even the bad guys and hired guns can escape the influence of Hollywood.

Crime School is at once serious, informative, fascinating and funny. There is another world out there that not many of us get to see, which "coppers" who are "on the job" are working hard to control. After you've read this book, you'll know what money laundering is, how it works, how it can be detected and how you can avoid being an unwitting accomplice in some unscrupulous money launderer's scheme.

Chris Mathers is an amazing guy, and *Crime School's* vivid and accurate depiction of the world of crime, criminals and policing reminded me why I had so many sleepless nights as Commissioner of the Royal Canadian Mounted Police.

Norman D. Inkster, Commissioner (Retired)
Royal Canadian Mounted Police (1987–1994)
President of Interpol (1991–1994)

ACKNOWLEDGMENTS

There's no way that I can list all of the people that helped make this book happen, either directly or just by being my friends. But I have to name a few.

At the publishers:
Michael Mouland, the supervising editor and my part-time scuba diving partner.

Lyn Cadence, director of publicity, and Clare McKeon, editor-in-chief, my friends and also big supporters of this project. And my editor, Doris Cowan, the world's foremost expert on punctuation, grammar and now.... money laundering.

At KPMG Forensic:
The members of the International Forensic Committee, Jim Hunter (Toronto), Petrus Marais (Cape Town), Rich Girgenti (New York), Adam Bates (London) and David Van Homrigh (Brisbane). Also Ellen Zimiles and Jim Mulvaney (New York), Nick Robinson (Hong Kong), Andre Fouche (Cape Town), Geronimo Timerman (Buenos Aires), Pablo Bernad (Madrid), Doug Tait (Bahrain) and Dave Potter (Amsterdam). A group of very talented people who have dedicated themselves to the detection of crime and who, collectively, have financed (perhaps unwittingly) most of my international travel over the past eight years.

On the Cayman Islands:
John Arnold, Theo Bullmore, Ian Comins, Paul Drake and Simon Whicker.

My oldest friend, ski buddy and car aficionado and, coincidentally the most dangerous contract lawyer I know, Lee Webster.

At Bank of America:
Ian Dear, for letting me photograph his money.

At the Canadian Bankers Association:
Ray Protti and Kelly Shaughnessy.

In law enforcement and intelligence:
Bernie Gold *(Raconteur, bon vivant, man about town.)*
Billy from the West Coast *(The FBI's favorite Mountie. An amazing talent.)*
Blackie *(Who shielded me from the brass and was last seen somewhere in Africa.)*
Carlo *(My Godfather and the personal bodyguard to Anne of Green Gables.)*
Coleman *(DEA's secret weapon who single-handedly lowered the crime rate in Nassau.)*
CW *(Formerly the tallest guy in Beijing.)*
Donny B. *(The "Warrior of the Wasteland" and my friend.)*
Elio *(Was Mr. Big, now he's Mr. Mom. A huge talent.)*
Fabrici *(The biggest G-Man in Frisco. In the "Jim," five days a week.)*
Gene *(Feared by the crooks. Loved by the cops, especially by me.)*
Home *(Cop, lawyer and talented pugilist.)*
Jeannette from L.A. *(Blonde, beautiful and still packing a machine-gun.)*
Jimmy the Boat *(Stones like a canal horse.)*

Monica *(Most of the guys couldn't carry her notebook.)*

Nick *(Friend, artist and boss who never lost confidence in me.)*

Pete *(The "Fighting Flight Attendant." A fearless cop.)*

Ray Hay *(The "Marathon Man.")*

Reid *(Former Spymaster and one of my favorite people.)*

Ricky *(The father of storefronts in Canada.)*

Rosemary *(The best-looking liaison officer in Europe.)*

Stevie *(My friend. A great investigator and now the boss!)*

Tattoo *(Saved my life in 1978 and responsible for it ever since.)*

The Man with the Plan *(My biggest supporter and the one who made everything happen for me.)*

The Other Nick *(Nick Denarco, the best blind undercover operator alive.)*

Tony from Miami *(Who will discover that life really begins at 50.)*

And to my family:
For putting up with me.

Chris

PREFACE

The price one pays for pursuing any profession or calling is an intimate knowledge of its ugly side.

JAMES BALDWIN
(1924–1987)

I am proud to say that for twenty years, I was a member of the Royal Canadian Mounted Police. For those of you not familiar with this organization, it's Canada's national police force: the guys with the red tunics, the Stetson hats and the horses. The RCMP is a peculiar law enforcement agency in that it has become an international symbol—a symbol of democracy. The familiar image of the big, handsome, square-jawed Canadian Mountie, arresting evildoers "in the name of the Queen," is a popular cultural icon. That image seemed to keep people happy enough. Crime, although taken seriously, wasn't something that really had an impact upon the average citizen's daily life.

But somewhere along the way, the world changed. Sadly, the day came when we all awoke to find that our beautiful country had lost its innocence. That what was once a law-abiding society in an unspoiled wilderness had acquired all the worst problems of modern urban society, including crime and terrorism.

So somebody decided that we should get rid of the horses and hire a few guys that maybe weren't so good-looking…and that's where I came in.

Besides being a national police force, the RCMP is Canada's Interpol representative agency. Its mandate is to fight crime inside the country and to work with law enforcement agencies around the world to combat crime that recognizes no national borders, except to find ways to profit by breaking the laws on both sides of those borders.

Most of my time as a police officer was spent working under-cover. At first, when I was young, I posed as an addict, buying dope on the street. As I grew older and learned more, so did the bad guys I was chasing, and as time passed I found myself concentrating mostly on organized crime. For the last several years of my career, I, along with colleagues from several other countries, operated a number of "front" businesses that we established in order to pose as money launderers.

Although I would like to be able to tell you the whole story of my adventures in those years, I can't. First, this book isn't an autobiography; it's about crime. Second, many years ago I signed a document that said that if I ever talk about anything that I'm not supposed to, the government has the right to throw me in jail and take away my birthday. But the most important reason is that these kinds of investigations are still going on in many countries and many of the techniques that I used are still in use today. Telling you certain operational details might be entertaining for you, but it would compromise ongoing cases and put friends of mine in a tight spot.

However, I can tell you that we traveled the world, met up with the bad guys and worked hard at convincing them we were their friends. We became their business associates, pretended to invest their money and then, when the time was right, we arrested them and turned their money over to Her Majesty or Uncle Sam. You also need to know that, as they say on *Dragnet*, some of the names have been changed to protect the innocent... which is me! It turns out that even if you're telling the truth, you can still be sued, so, in most cases, I gave the bad guys new names.

There are plenty of books out there that drone on and on about national and international legislation. I have tried to stay away from explaining the legal framework. This book will tell you about the *illegal* framework: how criminals actually operate, how organized crime is really set up and how the bad guys "launder" the dirty money that they make.

You need to know that although my parents raised me, the Mounted Police is where I grew up. Its members are my extended family.

I hope that, aside from learning a few things about crime, readers will come away from this book with some sense of the admiration and depth of affection that I have for those men and women. As you read this, they and their counterparts around the world are all still out there, putting themselves in harm's way.

This book is for them.

WHAT IS MONEY LAUNDERING?

The beginning of wisdom is to call things by their right names.

CHINESE PROVERB

I spent most of my adult life in the company of criminals. During that time, I learned how they operate but, more importantly, I learned how they perceive and take advantage of us, you and me, the so-called "straight" world. In my experience, neither regular citizens nor those employed in the financial industry really have a clue about what money laundering is or how investigators can follow the money trail to uncover many other types of crime.

People commit crimes for many reasons: love, hate, politics, revenge. But mostly, they do it for the money. Every time a crime is committed and money is generated, a bad guy is faced with a problem: how can he conceal the fruits of his crime? The bad guy wants to be able to spend his money without getting caught, and to do this, he needs to clean up the profits. He needs to launder the money. Money laundering means taking money derived from an illegal act and then putting it through a number of steps so that ultimately that same money appears to have been derived from something legitimate.

History of Money Laundering

The term "money laundering" was first coined in the 1930s by the U.S. Treasury agents who were trying to lock up Al Capone. In those days, very few people had running water, much less a washing machine, so commercial laundries were very common. Capone and his mob owned hundreds of laundries in and around Chicago, and they disguised the earnings from their liquor business as money honestly earned from operating the laundries. There were no U.S. statutes at that time that identified money laundering as an offense, but in the end, Capone was convicted of evading federal income tax. Tax evasion and money laundering are often very closely connected.

The U.S. was the first country to pass money laundering legislation, but they didn't really get around to investigating it until towards the end of the twentieth century. Everything changed when cocaine suddenly increased in popularity in North America. In the 1970s and early 1980s, its proximity to the source of the cocaine made south Florida the world center of money laundering activity.

At that point, money laundering became the flavor of the month. Everybody started talking about it, particularly politicians, most of whom didn't have a clue what it was in the first place.

Substantive Offenses

Without a crime, there is no money laundering. So money laundering investigations always have to start off by determining

One crime has to be concealed by another.
SENECA
(4 BC–65 AD)

the crime behind the money. This is known in legal circles as the "substantive offense."

The substantive offense can be any serious crime, but normally it's some kind of organized crime activity, such as drugs, fraud or theft. In recent years, with the increased focus on terrorism—what I like to call ideological crime—the substantive offense under investigation is more and more often one of violence. Although this can still mean traditional crimes involving violence, like extortion, armed robbery or kidnapping, the substantive offense that leads to money laundering can also be a conspiracy to commit a terrorist act. The people or governments that provide money to a terrorist organization to finance the terrorist act must launder it to conceal not only its source but also its purpose.

It also varies from country to country. In the United States, drug trafficking is considered to be the primary substantive offense to money laundering, whereas in a place like India, because of its foreign exchange controls, it's usually tax evasion.

It's normally not a big mystery where the money comes from, but it still has to be proven. For example, if the cops pull over a car full of illegal aliens from Colombia and find five million dollars in cash in the trunk, it's pretty obvious where the money came from. Nevertheless, they are required to show the nexus to drugs.

When I posed as a money launderer, it was always very important to prove, or somehow get the bad guys to admit, the illegal source of the money. We couldn't just ask, because that would have made them suspicious; in those days, before 9/11, real criminal money launderers couldn't have cared less whether you got your money from winning the lottery, selling drugs or robbing the poor box— and we were supposed to be real money launderers. But there was normally some parallel criminal case being investigated, most often drugs, which helped us prove that the money came from crime. If we were really lucky, when the bad guys brought us their money to be cleaned up or invested, it would turn out to be the actual cash that our undercover people had given them for a drug buy.

But life is rarely that simple. We usually had to get the bad guys to tell us. Please understand that I'm not giving away any big secrets here. Inasmuch as it used to be true that real criminal money launderers would rarely ask about the source of a bad guy's money, that all changed after 9/11. Terrorists and organized criminals are very similar and commit the same kinds of crimes; they also use the same money laundering organizations to look after their cash. But they are more dangerous clients for a money launderer to take on.

Why? Because when traditional law enforcement agencies investigate crimes, they are governed by the rule of law. Their ultimate goal is to convict the bad guys. The actions of law enforcement officers are closely controlled and scrutinized, and they are ultimately required to answer for all of their actions when they finally get into court. The bad guys know this, and they, and their defense lawyers, use it to their advantage.

But that was before terrorist money laundering became an issue.

Enter...the intelligence agencies. These guys operate from a different playbook. Their task is to protect the interests of the country. They don't go to court and they're not interested in making convictions. They just want to stop terrorists. So when those guys are interviewing a money launderer who has been involved with criminal and terrorist groups, you can be sure that the dynamics of the interview will be substantially different than it would be with the police. If you're moving money for a terrorist group and you don't cooperate with the intelligence agencies, you might wake up one morning and "not wake up." Money launderers know this, so, guess what, now they ask everybody where the money came from.

They don't always get an answer, though. Getting the bad guy to tell you where the cash came from can be a challenge.

Show Me the Money

The United States Bureau of Engraving and Printing unveiled a new $20 note on May 13, 2003 (see page 25). It has a large number of new features, most of them introduced for one reason only: to frustrate counterfeiters. But it will likely be years before all of the old $20 bills are recovered, so the bad guys still have some time to keep counter-

feiting the old notes before they have to start worrying. All in all, the twenty is a good-looking document, even if President Jackson does look like he "over-moussed."

What a lot of people don't know, however, is that the U.S. still has notes larger than the $100. They were last printed in 1945, but the Federal Reserve continued to issue them until 1969. There are very few, if any, in circulation these days, but they are still legal tender. After 1969, they were discontinued for "lack of use." Too bad for the currency smugglers. They would have loved a $10,000 bill.

The US$100,000 gold certificate (shown on page 27) was only used in the financial industry and was never in circulation as currency for public use. It's against the law for a private citizen to possess this note, even as a collector.

The $2 bill is another unusual American note. I don't know about you, but if I had been president, I'd be pretty unhappy about being stuck on the $2 bill. Although there are 583,045,729[1] of them out there, they are virtually uncirculated. Nobody asks for or uses them. People think they no longer exist. The $2 is not popular because at

one time the price of a prostitute was two dollars. Apparently men didn't want to hold them for fear people would think they associated with "ladies of the evening," and women didn't want to hold them for fear of being thought to be one.

Serious Money

Stick a few hundred dollars in twenties in your wallet and you'll start to understand the difficulties that dope dealers face when they have to store or transport their cash. Cash takes up a lot of space, and the older and more used it is, the more space it takes up. The picture below shows the difference between new and used bills. At first glance, it may seem that there's not a lot of difference, but this is only

$80,000 in twenties. Once you get into large amounts, the difference is impressive. In fact, the Bank of America people told me that many of their foreign clients prefer to buy new notes because of the extra weight involved in shipping used ones.[2]

The notes on the left are what are referred to as "Fed Fit," which means that it is new currency from the U.S. Federal Reserve and is hermetically sealed in plastic shrink wrap.

See the photo on page 29 if you want to know what $100,000 in $100 bills looks like. The label on these notes indicates that they were packaged at the Federal Reserve Bank in New York City and that there should be 1,000 notes, consecutively numbered, begin-

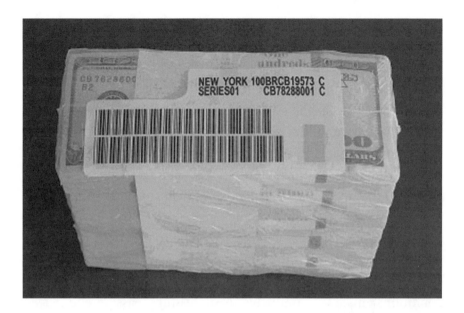

ning with CB 78288001. Quality control people at the mint check all of the notes and sometimes they will find a note that is misprinted. In that case, they just pull it and replace it with a spare, so sometimes you might find a note that is out of sequence in these packs.

A new U.S. dollar, right out of the mint, weighs about a gram. A million dollars weighs a lot—a *whole* lot if the denominations are small. Here's what a million dollars weighs, according to the type of bill:

$100 — 22 lbs
$ 50 — 44 lbs
$ 20 — 110 lbs
$ 10 — 220 lbs
$ 1 — 2,202 lbs

But criminals don't usually deal in new notes; they deal in used ones. Currency paper is 25 percent linen and 75 percent cotton, so notes get heavier as they are circulated because they absorb dirt and moisture along the way. So you can add as much as another 25 percent to these weights. The money that criminals are handling is usually large amounts of low-denomination notes because it comes from the sales of narcotics on the street. The denominations won't change that much as the money passes through the various levels of traffickers between the street and the people storing and transporting the money. So the people who have to move the money are dealing with huge numbers of notes that are heavy and take up a lot of space. U.S. currency measures 2.61 inches wide by 6.14 inches long and the thickness is .0043 inches.

Another problem that the bad guys have to deal with is counterfeit money. There's a ton of it out there, and the nature of drug trafficking (i.e., quick transactions that often take place in low-light conditions) makes it conducive to successfully passing counterfeit bills. A crackhead with access to a color photocopier would probably be able to get high for a considerable period of time before somebody caught on and cut his heart out.

When I ran undercover money laundering operations, we used to pass an ultraviolet light over the money to detect counterfeit. Those little detectors that you see in corner stores are based on the same principle: the paper that color photocopiers use iridesces under ultraviolet light, while real notes, with their cotton and linen composition, don't.

Bad guys always check for counterfeit, because it's a "heat score." The last thing they want is for the person or organization that is laundering their cash to have to answer questions about why there are counterfeit notes in the bundles.

Which brings me to another issue: how to prepare the cash. Most people, including drug dealers, seem to think that the money should be packaged in amounts, as opposed to denominations. Invariably, when we would start to deal with a new drug organization, I would have to sit down with them and explain how they should package the money to bring to us. It would usually take a few weeks or so for it to filter down through their entire organization.

We would explain to them that the bank likes the money in stacks of the same denomination, not a "party-pack" of fives, tens and twenties thrown together to make up a million. What lots of people also don't know, including most drug traffickers, it seems, is that banks will charge a "count fee" of as much as several hundred dollars on large amounts of cash. Even with counting machines, it takes a lot of time and effort to count cash, and the last they thing they need is to have to undo bundles and sort the notes before they count them. Besides, it just isn't professional.

Another problem is that, in some organizations, as the money gets moved up the line, everybody takes a little bit out for themselves. So by the time the money got to me, it would often be short several thousand dollars. I guess you really can't blame these guys for stealing a bit. After all, for the most part, you had guys from Jamaica, Colombia and other downtrodden places, who were probably the first people in their family tree to even wear shoes, and here they were counting and packaging millions of dollars in cash.

There was a time when drug trafficking groups were concerned about the presence of drug residue, particularly cocaine, on the notes. Years ago, before money laundering offenses were prosecuted as much as they are today, the cops used to send seized money to the crime lab to be analyzed for the presence of narcotics. If there was any residue, the money would be classified as drug money and impounded. This worked really well for a number of years, until one day, an enterprising young defense lawyer went to about ten different banks and sent random samples of currency to a private lab for drug testing. You guessed it, *all* of the randomly obtained money tested positive for narcotics as well. So that ended that.

I was once subpoenaed by a city police agency to give expert testimony on how money is packaged and transported by drug traffickers. The city cops had busted a hashish dealer, and besides the hash, they had discovered a suitcase with about $40,000 in it.

The way it works in court is that so-called expert evidence is really expert *opinion*. Now, normally you're not allowed to give your opinion in court, only facts. To do so, you need to be qualified by the court. This can be quite an onerous process for the expert, what with the prosecution standing up and telling the court what an ace you are and the defense countering with what a big loser you are and that you couldn't tell the truth with a gun to your head.

Anyway, this time the prosecution was able to overcome all odds and get me qualified. He then presented me with a big stack of fives, tens and twenties that were bundled up (very improperly and unprofessionally, I might add). I examined the money and, at one point, I smelled it. The exchange went something like this:

> *Prosecutor:* Why are you smelling the money?
> *Me:* To see if it smells like hashish.
> *Prosecutor:* And does it?
> *Defense:* Your honor!
> *Judge:* Don't answer that!
> *Prosecutor:* I'm sorry, your honor.

Of course the money smelled very strongly of hash, and the bad guy had probably stored the dope and the money together, as all not-so-smart dope dealers do. When the money was marked as an exhibit, it was placed in front of His Honor. During the rest of my testimony, I watched him out of the corner of my eye. I saw him pick up one of the bundles and casually smell it. The dealer pulled a nickel (received a five-year sentence).

The best way to get a bad law repealed is to enforce it strictly.

ABRAHAM LINCOLN
(1809–65)

The Financial Action Task Force

Every serious problem society faces, whether it's AIDS, homelessness, refugees or whatever, seems to give birth to an industry. Overnight, thousands of experts appear like magic, offering enlightened opinions on TV, writing hastily researched books* and organizing themselves into groups that "study" the problem or conduct "fact-finding missions." The main purpose often seems to be figuring out a way to get the government—actually the taxpayers—to pay for it. They also like issuing voluminous reports. (As a matter of fact, the most recent U.S. Senate Subcommittee Report on Correspondent Banking Practices and Money Laundering is currently supporting one corner of the couch in my basement.)

However, having said all that, the truth is that some groups actually serve a purpose. One of them is the Financial Action Task Force (FATF). The FATF is an organization of "developed" countries that have banded together under the auspices of the Organization for Economic Co-operation and Development (OECD) in an attempt to combat international money laundering. In June 2000, after an investigation that included visiting countries that were considered money laundering locales, they issued a "blacklist" of fifteen countries that they felt were not doing enough to prevent money laundering in their jurisdictions. These countries were:

Bahamas	Nauru
Cayman islands	Nive
Cooks Islands	Panama
Dominica	Philippines
Israel	Russia
Lebanon	St. Kitts and Nevis
Liechtenstein	St. Vincent and the
Marshall Islands	Grenadines

* Well, except for this book, of course!

What the FATF said was that these countries fell short of international standards in that they had "insufficient or non-existent legislation to combat money laundering." For example, they had no laws against corporate structures that permitted the concealment of the identity of the beneficial owner. All of the UN countries were advised that they should provide "closer scrutiny" to all transactions involving the blacklisted countries. The countries on the blacklist were told that they had better get their houses in order quick or they would face "sanctions." Now, no one ever came right out and said exactly what those sanctions would be, but the rumor is that there was talk of restricting air traffic, refusing to accept wire transfers, even an out-and-out naval blockade. Most of the countries got going on this right away, except for the tiny South Pacific island of Niue, whose authorities didn't even reply to the FATF's letter. Maybe they never got it?

Every year or so, the FATF makes changes to its list to reflect which countries have been naughty or nice. If you go to their website at www1.oecd.org/fatf/, you can view the current list.

In spite of being part of the huge bureaucracy of the OECD, the FATF is an effective organization. They do good work and they are making headway in the fight against money laundering. However, they have made a few decisions that I find a bit confusing. Such as removing Russia from the list of non-cooperating countries. It appears that, for some countries, all you have to do to get taken off the list is pass some money laundering laws. You don't actually have to enforce them, just pass them.

ORGANIZED CRIME

Organized crime in America takes in over $40 billion a year. This is quite a profitable sum, especially when one considers that the Mafia spends very little for office supplies.

WOODY ALLEN
(1935–)

Organized crime is everywhere. We rub up against it every single day of our lives and most people never even notice. It affects everything that we do.

Think about a typical day in your own life. You get up in the morning and you get dressed. You put on that new shirt that you just bought and a button pops off it as you do it up. You paid $150 for that shirt, because it was made in Italy by a famous designer. You paid more for it because of the name. What you don't know is that the shirt wasn't manufactured in Italy but in Southeast Asia, at a factory controlled by an Asian organized crime group that manufactures knock-offs of everything from Rolex to Louis Vuitton.

You get into your car and you drive to work. Traffic is terrible. A car has broken down and is blocking traffic. The engine has stalled because there is dirt in the gas line. The car's owner bought gas at a small gas station that purchases its product from a company that is controlled by organized crime. And these organized crime guys buy low-quality fuel, smuggle it into your country and sell it at a reduced price to small independents, who sell it to you.

A little later on, traffic slows again. Construction on the highway: they're resurfacing the road. The contractors who were originally awarded the paving contract had mob connections and were able to rig the bids in the tender process so they came in with the lowest price. But, to make money at that price, they only put down half an inch of asphalt instead of the full inch that they were supposed to.

When the inspector from the city came to check the quality of the work, they gave him $500 to look the other way.

You finally get to work, but you're late and the parking lot beneath your office is full. You have to park at another lot. They want to charge you $30 to park for the day. You tell the parking guy to forget it and you go to the next lot down the street. The next parking guy, who coincidentally looks and talks very much like the first parking guy, tells you in very broken English that the price is $30 there, too. The company that runs the lot has had to put up their prices. Almost all of their employees are members of the same ethnic group; in fact, many of them are related to each other. The employees have discovered a way to subvert the parking payment system. They're stealing millions of dollars each year. As well, although it normally costs a monthly fee of $250 to park there, for $500 the parking guy will give you a bootleg pass card that will work for a whole year.

Some of the profits that parking attendants have made from this scam are being used to bribe a visa control officer at Canada's embassy in their home country, so that more of their clan, many with serious criminal records, can get into the country ahead of legitimate immigrants (some of whom have been waiting for years).

When you finally get to the office, there are three voicemails from your boss, looking for a report that you were supposed to have sent him by email yesterday. But the email is down. One of your employees was downloading porno films onto his laptop at home last night; he picked up a virus, which he spread to the entire network when he signed on at the office this morning.

"Can't we fax it?" you scream. Sorry, boss, no can do. Someone in purchasing tried to save money by buying recycled cartridges that were offered over the telephone by a "boiler-room" operation (high-pressure phone sales pitches coming to you from an unknown location). The cartridges screwed up the fax machine.

The mailroom delivers your mail and there's a special package for you. It's big and heavy and it's from the mobile phone company. Is it that new phone upgrade that you've been waiting for? No, it's your bill. Somebody "cloned" your mobile phone and has been renting it out for the past thirty days to people who want to call China.

Time to check the stock prices. More bad news. That stock that your brother-in-law got the hot tip on—the one you bought with the money you were supposed to spend on a new dining-room suite—just ceased trading, after the price started dropping like a stone. Apparently some mob guys were running a "pump and dump" operation: after artificially inflating the price of the stock, they sold it all, taking your investment as profit.

You're feeling stressed. You need a cigarette. You know that you really should quit, because the price of cigarettes keeps going up. But the guy at the corner store near your office buys them on the Indian reserve, where an organized crime group smuggles them in across the border, without paying any duties or taxes. So you step outside for a smoke.

You have an important appointment with a client and you decide to take her to a very expensive restaurant for lunch. After a nice meal and two bottles of wine, you ask for the check. The waiter tells you that your credit card has been declined. The client ends up having to pay the bill. Turns out that you were the victim of identity theft. Some bad guys used your name and applied for credit, running up bills in the thousands. The credit-reporting agency, on the advice of the bank, suspended your card.

This whole thing is giving you heartburn. Must have been all the pepperoni that you had on that pizza last night. (More about that later.) You've been taking prescription antacids that your doctor prescribed, but they don't seem to work. That's because they were made for the drug manufacturer by a subcontractor in Indonesia. The factory, which uses children and convicts as laborers, is operated by organized crime, and they've been diluting the medication with chalk.

Finally, your workday ends. Back into another traffic jam. This time, there's a guy standing beside a car stalled in the center lane. The garage that replaced the guy's fuel injection system used counterfeit parts, which failed after about six months. You finally get past the guy, but then a piece of concrete from the overpass falls off and lands on the hood of your car. Guess what? The same company that got the paving contract also built the overpass.

You won't even bother making an insurance claim. Insurance fraud by organized crime has driven the cost of car insurance up so high that your deductible is now almost two grand! You get home late. Your wife is crying. Your sixteen-year-old son got caught smoking pot at school. All you can say is—where did he get it?

You can't take it anymore. You head for your favorite bar. But it's closed, out of business. It seems that they just couldn't compete with the bar across the street—a new place where they don't seem to be that interested in making a profit. Why? Because it's owned by the organization that imported the pot that your son got caught with, and they are using the bar to launder the proceeds of their drug sales.

You throw up your hands and go home. You finally settle down and put your feet up. Time to watch TV. You've got the latest counterfeit version of the decoding chip for your satellite dish, which you buy from the guy at the electronics store in the mall. But the only thing that's on is *The Sopranos*.

The doorbell rings. It's your brother-in-law, the genius who gave you the stock tip. He had a job with a legitimate highway contractor, but because those other crooked contractors made such great profits doing inferior work, he lost his job...

So now he's moving in with you.

Organized crime touches us all every day...in ways that perhaps you never even considered.

All Mobbed Up and No Place to Go

When you hear the word "Mafia," chances are the first image that comes into your mind is a movie actor. Probably somebody like Al Pacino or James Gandolfini. That's because most people's perception of crime and criminality is shaped by popular culture; by films and television.

And you're not the only one influenced by Hollywood. Crooks don't have that many role models, so they often take their behavioral clues from the media as well. You'll often hear young Italian guys from Seattle or Toronto affecting accents that make them sound like they're from the Bronx.

In 1991, in the popular crime film *Boyz N the Hood*, the bad guys were depicted holding their guns sideways. It was the first time this image showed up on a movie screen. Why were they holding their guns sideways? Because the actors thought it looked cool, that's why. And believe me, being cool is very important to bad guys, too. Since that time, the protagonists of countless motion pictures have been filmed holding their guns sideways, and now, if you look at videos of real bank robberies, you'll see that the bandits will often hold their guns in the same fashion. There's no advantage in doing this. You certainly can't shoot better. It just looks cooler. (Incidentally, I went out to the range one day and tried to shoot like this. It's hard to do. I almost shot a hole in the car.)

Some years ago, a bank called the police because they thought they had spotted a pair of money launderers. An old Italian guy had come into the branch with a younger, well-dressed bodyguard type. As they waited for the teller, the bodyguard kept going to the front window of the bank and looking up and down the street—obviously, checking for heat (police surveillance or attention).

The old Italian man removed close to half a million dollars from a bag and says to the teller that he wants to open an account and make a deposit. The money was old, some of it moldy and dirty. The teller was convinced that it was loot from some old bank robbery or kidnapping. She alerted the manager, who called the police.

What was really happening was this: the old guy was the grandfather, the "bodyguard" was, in reality, his grandson. The grandson had been visiting, and discovered that the old man had been hiding money all over his house and had even been burying it in the backyard. The young man was afraid, and with good reason. The formerly traditional Italian immigrant neighborhood where the grandfather lived had over the years been taken over by crackheads and prostitutes, and was now a dangerous place for an old man living alone. So the grandson finally convinced the old boy, who "didn't trust banks," that he had to secure his money. And that's why they were at the bank that day.

But what about the "bodyguard" acting nervous and keeping an eye on the street? Well, it turns out that he had parked his car in a no-stopping zone and was afraid of getting towed.

So what's the point of this story? What it means is that when people try to pick out the bad guys, they're usually looking for Don Corleone, when maybe they should be looking for Don Knotts.

And that's the key. Criminals look like you and me. They aren't going to look like the bad guys you see in the movies.

Casinos

Another misconception movie audiences tend to take home is that money laundering is something that happens in casinos. In reality, unless you own the casino, it's a pretty bad place to try and launder money.

Years ago, when organized crime controlled all of the casinos in Las Vegas, there was probably a fair amount of it, but in those days they also had what was known as the "skim." The skim meant removing money off the top of the profits and concealing it from the IRS. But if they were doing that, they also had to launder the skim somehow, which pretty well negates the whole idea of injecting extra cash into the gross profits. Most of the time, though, when people talk about laundering money through a casino, they mean people coming in and buying chips with cash, the idea being that they would play the tables for a while and then cash in their chips and ask for a check in return. Supposedly, they would then take that check and deposit it into a bank account as the first step of the money laundering process, the so-called placement stage.

The truth is, if you are planning to try to launder money through a casino, you will get pinched. Next time you're in a casino, look around. More importantly, look up. All you will see anywhere are those black globes: the ones that contain the video cameras. Mostly, they're looking for cheaters, card counters, card sharps and the like. But they are also looking for anything out of the ordinary. Casinos operate on a license, and they are not about to lose it because some dope dealer decided that he was going to start using their joint as his personal laundromat.

The casino business prides itself on customer service. They know their customers' habits, and that's how they do what they do. A "whale"* is definitely not going to show up with a suitcase full of cash. Everything is done by bank transfer or line of credit. A big player in a casino will always have an established line of credit, backed by a bank. Anybody who shows up with a whole whack of cash and tries to buy chips is going to be asked to fill in a form declaring the source of the funds before he gets to play. So that screws that up.

The next technique would be to send confederates in individually

---

* A "whale" is a casino term for a big spender, who is prepared to drop hundreds of thousands of dollars in a very short time. In Las Vegas and Atlantic City, casino managers cater to the whales. They are supplied with private aircraft, limousines, private tables and all of the other "perks" that the casino trade has to offer.

to buy chips with smaller amounts of cash. Those chips would eventually be cashed in by one guy, who would ask for some type of check or draft. This would work, but all in all, it's a very unwieldy process, and if you did it more than a couple of times, you would end up in chains.

One more thing: although the casinos are in competition with each other, the security people all seem to get along famously. And they're pretty much all ex-cops. So if somebody starts trying to launder money on the strip, everybody will know about it within days and likely have a picture of the guy as well.

Outlaw Motorcycle Gangs

There are tons of biker gangs out there around the world. The Hells Angels, Outlaws, Bandidos, etc., are active in most of the industrialized Western countries. They are a curious organized crime group in that they don't operate like other groups in a variety of ways. The first and most obvious difference is that they often wear a huge sign on their backs that shouts, "Hey, look at me. I'm a criminal." Despite this bizarre behavior, they are highly organized and sophisticated in many ways.

Biker gangs don't deal drugs. Bikers deal drugs. Certain members of the club simply use the club structure and some of its members to carry out their task. Most gangs couldn't put a pound of grass together if you relied on the gang as an entity to do so.

Consider the example of two members of a biker gang trafficking in cocaine. They sell drugs as a team because they are friends. They may obtain their drugs from other bikers in another location, but chances are they have their own connection. And they get other people to do all the things that you go to jail for if you get caught, like making deliveries and collecting debts. For such menial tasks, our two bikers would make use of women and "strikers"—probationary members of the club who have not yet passed their initiation. As such, they are obliged to act virtually as indentured servants to full-fledged club members.

This kind of arrangement allows a sophisticated drug trafficker to avoid actually handling the product—unless it's to stick his nose in the bag. The myth perpetuated by popular culture that high-level traffickers rarely use their product is exactly that—a myth. Most drug traffickers use it a lot. In fact, one of the common ways of getting caught by the police (or murdered by your colleagues) is to use too much of your own product.

The reality is that very few other members of the club will know anything about the activities of the two bikers who are selling drugs, other than that they are doing it. Most bikers know from personal experience that everyone in the club is a potential "rat." Also, although everyone pays dues to keep the group running, it's not like the traditional Italian organized crime "families," where members of the gang are obliged to "kick up" a percentage of whatever they earn to their bosses. In most biker gangs, it's every man for himself. Successful entrepreneurs like our two dealers might be expected to sponsor a party or some kind of gathering at least once during the year. But that's about as far as it goes.

Strip Clubs and Brothels

Bikers, especially the ones who sell drugs, are fond of establishing legitimate, cash-intensive businesses so they can launder the fruits of their illegal activities. They are particularly entrenched in the strip club industry. In fact, until a few years ago, outlaw motorcycle gangs controlled the majority of the strippers in North

Vice is its own reward.
The Naked Civil Servant (1968)
QUENTIN CRISP
(1908–99)

America. That changed with the arrival of Russian organized crime. Russian strippers can now be found in almost every city in the free world where that kind of thing is allowed.

This is an area of the entertainment business that is not only profitable but provides a ready-made platform to launder illegal money. Some organized crime groups own the strip bars; others are happy to simply represent the "talent." Either way, it's a cash cow. The regular patrons that these kinds of places attract are quite often the same people who purchase drugs or visit prostitutes. For them, it's kind of like one-stop shopping.

It's a pretty simple matter to inject the illegal cash proceeds from drugs and sex into the legal proceeds of a strip bar. The bar generates cash like any other business and the illegal cash can be easily commingled with the normal income.

The strippers themselves are part of a complex symbiotic relationship with the crooks. They are often under the thumb of the bad guys, and, because of this, they are required to give up a good portion of their money to them. In return, they get protection, transportation and a bit of management. The ones that are also working as hookers (and there are many that are) usually do the same, and the amount of money that they get to keep for themselves varies from group to group. But it's never very much.

In the case of Russians and other foreign strippers and hookers, they are usually new to the country and completely controlled by the bad guys. You'll often read stories in the papers about how these women were tricked into leaving their home countries to travel overseas to become models or entertainers. Don't believe it. The majority of them know exactly what they are coming over to do. In fact, many of them were hookers in their home countries before making the trip. But that doesn't make a very interesting story, and it also disappoints all the social activists who feed off this kind of thing.

However, the social activists are right about one thing: these women may have known what they were going to be doing, but not many are prepared for the working conditions that they will encounter. Asian organized groups often smuggle women into the country in the same fashion that illegal immigrants are brought in. In the case of traditional human smuggling, migrants pay the snakeheads a substantial sum of money, often as much as $25,000, to come to North America. "Snakehead" is a rather ominous term used to describe the leader of a human smuggling ring. (The term appears to be derived from the image of the person at the head of a long line of people moving across a border.) Most of these people land in Canada and then slip across the border into the United States. But not the sex trade workers. For a start, they rarely have any money. The criminals who bring them in usually make them service the debt by servicing customers. The crooks will normally hold their passports and keep them "sequestered," in reality imprisoned, in a "safe" house. They are not allowed to leave without an escort, and it's not uncommon for them to work for a couple of years before they can work off the money that their masters claim they owe.

Over the years, I've raided a number of brothels and massage parlors (known in the vernacular as "rub-'n'-tug," the massage part being the "rub" and the sex part being the "tug") that were run by the Vietnamese and Chinese gangs. The conditions were squalid; several girls to a room and not much room, or time, for personal hygiene.

One of my informants ran a number of these places. Some of these girls were handling a dozen customers a day. My informant was in the practice of giving his girls antibiotics regularly, but not out of any sense of compassion. The antibiotics didn't protect the girls, they simply masked any primary symptoms of gonorrhea that might have been evident. The girls were not all that well educated and usually didn't protect themselves. I once asked one of them about condoms. She said, "If man want, we use." AIDS was just starting to make an appearance in North America back then. Nobody had any idea how bad things were going to get.

The money generated by the sex trade is substantial, particularly in the Asian community, where there are large numbers of men who have come to North America to try and earn enough money to bring their families over. This cash is washed through a variety of legitimate businesses. Add to that the fact that the Asian community operates very much on a cash basis, and the problem of disposing of the criminal proceeds is pretty well dealt with.

The informant that I mentioned was a cab driver as well as a pimp; that's how he laundered the proceeds from his brothels. Although he spent a lot of the cash just living, he simply declared all the rest on his income tax. The tax man didn't seem to care that a cab driver was pulling down a couple of hundred thousand a year, as long as he was getting his "end." (An "end," or a "piece," is a share of the profits of a deal.)

This guy was the most pragmatic person I have ever encountered. He once described to me, with about as much emotion as somebody complaining about a bad haircut, how his mother had been murdered by some Portuguese guy in New York. Some months later, he was having trouble with a Vietnamese gangster. Apparently, some of the Vietnamese gang members had been to my guy's brothels and had been causing trouble, fooling around with the girls and refusing to pay. Things escalated and they kidnapped some of his girls and also his wife. These things are never reported to the police, but the rumor was that they held them at some motel for a while, had their way with all of them and then let them go.

A few Fridays later, at about 4 a.m., the gang leader, another guy and a woman were coming out of a club. Two guys with machine-guns walked up to them and shot the three of them to pieces. The guns, two balaclavas and some earplugs were all left at the scene or close by. Interestingly, it appeared that one of the shooters threw up at the scene. One of them must have been a young kid, "making his bones." The local cops never solved the murders. The rumor was that the shooters were from New York.

The Bankruptcy of Murder, Incorporated

On TV or in the movies, people are always getting shot. The average person probably witnesses several thousand serious acts of violence every year, just sitting in his or her living room—even more if they turn the TV on. We are constantly reading or hearing of new reports and studies showing that people, especially young people, are becoming desensitized to violence because they are exposed to it every time they switch on the tube. This may be true, but, desensitized or not, most young people are not out in the streets lighting each other up.

> There's nothing wrong with shooting, as long as the right people get shot.
> DIRTY HARRY
> (CLINT EASTWOOD)
> (1930–)

To "light someone up" is a slang term used by criminals and usually means fatally shooting someone. Within the black or the I-wanna-be-black criminal element, they prefer the more poetic "bust a cap," which literally means to discharge a bullet, or "bust a cap in your ass," which doesn't always mean that you are going to get a bullet in your butt, it just means that you're going to get shot. Personally, I prefer the old-fashioned terms Philip Marlowe used: when somebody got shot, he was "ventilated" or "aired out."

But whatever you call it, violence is pervasive in the drug trade. It's much more obvious at the street level, because when one crack dealer knocks off another, it's not usually done with any finesse. In less developed countries, the violence between powerful criminal groups is often confused with political factional disputes. At that level, crime, terror and politics are often one and the same and people are always getting killed. Think about it; even with a war on, there were still drug traffickers in Sarajevo. In the middle of all of that violence, it would be easy to knock off the competition and blame it on the war. Besides, there is little or no law enforcement activity in those countries anyway.

In the movies, when someone gets shot, they usually fall down dead right away or they bravely hold a bandage to their wound and keep on fighting, acting as if they've done nothing more than broken a nail. This is far from the truth. In my experience, when somebody gets shot, they make a lot of noise, because it really hurts.

And for another thing, in real life, most people actually do get shot in the butt. The reason for this is pretty simple. The minute they see a gun, most people do the smart thing: they turn and start running. When you hear about cops getting shot in the leg or the ever-popular "lower back," it usually means they took one in the ass diving under a car.

For criminals, particularly the younger ones, the prospect of getting into a gun battle with the police is pretty scary. In the early 1990s, some city cop friends of mine were making cases against Chinese street gangs that were doing smash-and-grabs at jewelry stores. (As the term suggests, a "smash-and-grab" is a short, speedy theft or robbery in which a store window or interior display case is smashed and the goods taken.) The gangs were ultra-violent and weren't above shooting it out with the cops or other gangs. Apparently, the gang was getting ready to do a "score" (a criminal act, usually theft or robbery), when a fifteen-year-old kid who was going to be used as a six-man (a lookout—the job is referred to as "keeping" or "standing six") started to cry. When one of the older gang guys asked him what his problem was, he replied that he was afraid of getting shot. The other guy told him not to worry about it, because getting shot didn't really hurt all that much. The kid replied that he didn't believe him, so the older gang guy pulled out a pistol, shot him in the thigh and said, "You see, it doesn't hurt that much."

Although a few criminals carry guns all the time, most don't. There are a number of reasons for this. First of all, guns are heavy. If it isn't heavy, you shouldn't be carrying it anyway because it probably won't do the job. But because it's heavy, it's a pain to carry around; so unless they have a reason for it, they'll leave it at home. It's very much like carrying a big hammer around with you all of the time. Unless you have to drive some nails, it's useless.

Second, unlike in the movies, very few criminals wear a rig (gun holster), so they are obliged to stick the gun in their waistband. It's very uncomfortable, especially if you've got a bit of a belly, and the gun will often slip out, go down your pant leg and fall out on the floor. It can be very embarrassing, and criminals don't want to look like dorks any more than the rest of us. Only once did I ever see a crook with a respectable rig, and it turned out that both the gun and the holster had been stolen from a policeman's house.

Accidents can happen to the cops, too. I know of someone from a federal law enforcement agency (which will remain nameless) who accidentally shot himself with a .45 when he tried to carry it in his waistband in the small of his back. The bullet went in through one of his butt cheeks and out the other, ultimately earning him the nickname "Three-Hole."

Another thing is, guns are expensive. Depending on your status in the underworld, you may be sharing the gun with others, so you can't carry it all of the time. In fact, I knew of this old guy in Montreal who used to rent guns and other equipment to guys who wanted to do scores. For most bad guys, though, using someone else's gun is like wearing someone else's bathing suit. You just don't feel comfortable.

Finally, unless you have a reason to carry a gun—such as a drug deal or a robbery—it's better to keep it "laid down" (concealed in a secret location). If the cops take you off, suspecting you're a "Bernie" (an NYPD expression that means a white man carrying a gun. The reference is to Bernard Goetz, the infamous subway vigilante), and they find you really are packing a gun, you're going to pull some time. Also, if it's a "communal" firearm, that is, one that's being used by a number of people, you may be holding a gun that was used in a homicide; in which case, to paraphrase Ricky Ricardo, "You got some 'splainin' to do."

In the movies and on TV, international assassins fly around the world on the Concorde, have sex with supermodels and eliminate their victims using sophisticated technology. They then collect a huge fee. In real life, people that kill people for other people are usually either very dumb, very stoned or very crazy. As for being paid a lot of money, most of these guys are lucky to get carfare. In the underworld, murdering someone on behalf of another is usually something that one does to garner favor with that particular person. Money rarely changes hands. The shooter is usually just playing for "shape." (This is a term used in billiards that refers to positioning the cue ball to put yourself in a better situation for your next shot. On the street, "playing for shape" refers to trying to gain favor with another person, usually someone of higher status.)

The only people that offer "hit men" $50,000 are idiotic business tycoons who have seen too many films and want to murder their wives; they usually find out at the end that the hit man they've just hired to commit murder is an undercover police officer.

Art Appreciation

Because it's getting tougher and tougher to launder your money, crooks are always looking for new ways to conceal and convert their wealth, as well as novel ways to safely and secretly transmit it to the other people with whom they transact business.

> If all mankind were suddenly to practice honesty, many thousands of people would be sure to starve.
>
> G. C. LICHTENBERG
> *(1742–99)*

And since most drug traffickers are not accustomed to the lifestyles of the rich and famous, they all seem to have a need to spend their money on things that make them feel more sophisticated; things like fine wines, jewelry, luxury cars, racehorses and, of course, art. By buying this stuff, they feel that they're more able to fit in with all the rich people who got their money in more traditional ways, like inheriting it from their parents.

Some years ago, some agents of a U.S. federal agency busted this big dope dealer who had a number of residences, including a ranch. There were several very expensive racehorses on the ranch, so two agents were left to look after them for a few days until the U.S. marshals could get there and process everything as seized property. Trouble was, the two agents were from New York or Newark or someplace like that and they didn't know anything about horses. But they knew horses ate oats, so that's what they gave them. Whether you like them or not, horses are pretty dumb, and these ones were no exception. They ate all the oats that the agents left and drank all the water they could. By the time the marshals got there, the horses' stomachs were so swollen that they were almost touching the ground. As far as I know, none of them died, but they probably didn't win many races after that.

Next to racehorses, there's nothing like art to crank up your snob appeal. Many people pretend to know something about it, but few really do, and that includes most customs officers. So if you need to get a large amount of money across a border, it's not that difficult to smuggle an item worth millions without the authorities detecting its value. Another advantage is that the art world has an extensive gray market as well as a black market. (In the gray market, transactions are frequently done in cash to avoid tax. In the black market, transactions are frequently done in cash to avoid getting arrested.)

Art appreciates in value very quickly sometimes. I was involved in a case recently where a guy ripped off his employer for several million dollars and used some of the money to buy art. The rest of the money? He spent it on his girlfriend, of course! In this case, the employer lucked out. Turns out that one of the paintings that the bad guy bought was by a fairly famous artist. During the time it was in the thief's possession, the artist died. Dying has always been a good career move in the art world. The painting doubled in value overnight, and so, when we eventually seized it from the bad guy, we were able to recover substantially more of the money than we had first hoped.

> Certain criminal elements might even consider stolen artwork as a new form of currency.
>
> DAVID SCULLY
> *Underwriting Director,*
> *AXA Art Insurance Corporation*

For drug traffickers, paying for a drug shipment with a work of art is a rather efficient way of doing business. Let's say you owe your supplier five million for your last cocaine shipment. You know that he is interested in art and, by coincidence, you recently acquired a couple of Salvador Dalí oils and a Picasso pencil sketch from one of your customers as payment for a $250,000 drug debt. All three are obviously stolen, but your supplier doesn't mind. He is going to hang them on the wall of his villa in Baranquilla; not much chance of Interpol spotting them there. Your customer settled a $250,000 drug debt with three works of art that he probably got for very little money, since either he, or someone who works for him, stole them.

You, in turn, have settled a $5-million debt with your supplier with paintings that you got for $250,000. Truth is, drug trafficking and money laundering are believed to be partly responsible for a marked increase in art theft worldwide.[3]

Internationally, there is a huge traffic in stolen works of art. Criminals are at the front of the line to buy whatever they can, and despite being "nouveau riche," wealthy criminals can sometimes be

quite discriminating in their taste in art. The late Pablo Escobar, for example, the most high-profile member of the infamous Medellin Cartel, furnished all of his homes with expensive paintings and, curiously, developed a special interest in Chinese porcelain. Not bad for a guy who started his criminal career stealing tombstones, sanding off the deceased's names and then reselling them.[4]

The painting in the picture on page 53, being held by an El Salvadorean police officer, is believed to have once belonged to Pablo Escobar. It was seized in 1996 after the cops interrupted a drug transaction in a restaurant in San Salvador. It appeared that the painting was to be used as payment for a drug shipment. The art expert who examined it believes that it may in fact be a Picasso, but although signed, it was undated.[5] It's hard to say how it ended up in the restaurant...and Escobar isn't saying.

It can be very embarrassing for the artists themselves that their works have become one of the new currencies in the drug trade. Fernando Botero, the well-known Colombian artist, was particularly enraged when the Colombian police seized two of his paintings hanging in one of Escobar's homes. He was quoted in the national newspaper as saying, "I feel repugnance that my name should be linked to Pablo Escobar's because of those paintings. I did not sell them to him or know they were there."[6]

In January 2003, Colombian police arrested Joaquin Mario Valencio Trujillo, a.k.a. "El Joven" ("the youngster"). Valencio Trujillo is a well-known horse breeder in Colombia who somehow ended up marrying Luz Mery Tristan, a former competitive speed skater. He is alleged to have been a partner of the Rodriguez-Orejuela brothers of the Cali Cartel. The DEA allege that Valencio Trujillo "controlled most of the drug trafficking and money laundering operations in Colombia."[7] In addition to the 285 horses seized, which were worth as much as $500,000 each, Colombian police seized a total of fifty-four works of art and four armored cars.

General Noriega's Kingdom

And then there's General Manuel Noriega, convicted drug trafficker, CIA informant and former president of Panama. Noriega had more than fifty paintings in just one of his condos. Of course, most of them didn't count since they were painted on black velvet. But Noriega had other ways to launder drug money, of which he had plenty.

In August 1989, Lawrence Eagleburger, the acting U.S. Secretary of State, in a speech to the Organization of American States (OAS), shed some light on the nature of General Noriega's activities and the source and size of his wealth. Noriega had been indicted a year earlier, in 1988, along with Escobar and other members of the Medellin Cartel, but he hadn't been arrested yet and was still running Panama.

The indictments against Noriega that Eagleburger mentioned included:

- The attempted importation into the United States of over a million pounds of marijuana during 1983–84.
- Transporting millions of dollars in U.S. currency (representing the proceeds from the successful importation of 280,000 pounds of marijuana into the United States) to Panama to be laundered through Panamanian banks and businesses, with the approval and assistance of [Noriega].
- Facilitating the importation of 400,000 pounds of marijuana into the United States and the laundering of more than $100 million in illicit proceeds through Panama.
- Receiving payments of approximately $1 million for authorization and approval of marijuana smuggling and money laundering activities within Panama.
- Exploiting his official position as head of the intelligence section of the National Guard of Panama and then as

commander in chief of the Panama Defense Forces (PDF) to receive payoffs in return for assisting and protecting international drug traffickers.

- Assisting in the conduct of narcotics and money laundering operations in Panama, which included Pablo Escobar Gaviria, Gustavo DeJesus Gaviria Rivero, Jorge Ochoa Vasquez and Fabio Ochoa Vasquez [essentially, the whole Medellin Cartel].
- Protecting cocaine shipments flown from Medellin, Colombia, through Panama to the United States.
- Arranging for the transshipment and sale of ether and acetone, including such chemicals previously seized by the PDF, to the Medellin Cartel.
- Providing refuge and a base for continued operations to the members of the Medellin Cartel after the murder of the Colombian minister of justice, Rodrigo Lara Bonilla, in 1984.
- Agreeing to protect a cocaine laboratory being constructed in Darien Province, Panama.
- Assuring the safe passage of millions of dollars of narcotics proceeds into Panamanian banks.
- Receiving more than $4.6 million from the members of the Medellin Cartel in exchange for services rendered.
- Complicity in the importation of more than one ton of cocaine into Miami, Florida, on June 15, 1984.[8]

With all of his criminal activities, it's a wonder that Noriega ever found time to run the country. And he was making an absolute fortune. At the height of his activities, the U.S. government estimated Noriega's personal wealth at approximately $300 million, most of which was squirreled away in tax havens, far from Panama. From what I've heard, I think that it was probably much more than that.

Panama is one of the few countries in the world that recognizes Taiwan as a sovereign state. In fact, there's a huge Taiwanese population in Panama; for years, planeloads of Taiwanese visitors arrived almost every day at the airport in Panama. In fact, just after General Pizza Face got his free trip to Florida, I was down in Panama City and I met a guy who told me that, for a payment of about $30,000 to the "Noriega Retirement Fund," many of those Taiwanese "tourists" were obtaining resident status in Panama. Admittedly, my source had a bit of an ax to grind, since Noriega had him arrested, but I believe what he said was true. And if you do the math, it's a huge amount of money.

In the same speech to the OAS, Acting Secretary Eagleburger went on to describe some of El Presidente's personal holdings:

- A luxurious $600,000 mansion in Panama City hung with nearly fifty valuable oil paintings, and a chalet near a Panamanian air strip in Rio Hato.
- A vacation home on Madden Lake, and a mountain retreat with a mansion and several houses on sixty acres in Chiriqui Province, Panama.
- A farm in France, approximately fifty minutes from Paris, and a luxury apartment in an elite section of Paris.
- Several luxury apartments in the Dominican Republic, where Noriega's wife purchased furniture, art objects and antiques valued in the millions of dollars.
- Various jet aircraft, including three Lear jets and a twin-engine aircraft. In 1984 he purchased a sophisticated helicopter for his personal use for $2 million. In late 1983, Steven Kalish (who was indicted with Noriega on the importation of 280,000 pounds of marijuana into the U.S.) negotiated and purchased a Boeing 727 jet aircraft for $2.2 million for Noriega; the jet was later used for money laundering.

- An account at the Panama City branch of the Bank of Credit and Commerce International, with a balance of between $20 million and $25 million at various times.
- Three large pleasure yachts—the *Macho I, Macho II* and *Macho III.*

"*Macho I*"? Give me a break. This just goes to show that you can be hugely wealthy, the leader of a country and a huge dork, all at the same time. Anyway, spending money must have run in the family. Noriega, his wife and their three daughters were regular guests at the Helmsley Palace Hotel and ran up huge hotel bills. José Blandon, the former Panamanian consul general in New York, told the U.S. government that one of Noriega's daughters spent more than $50,000 during a one-day shopping trip to New York.[9]

Panama is a beautiful country and, since the departure of Noriega, they have been doing their best to get rid of corruption, but the signs of the drug trade are everywhere. Below is a shot of the waterfront in Panama City. As you can see, there are plenty of condos there, far too many for a place like Panama City. The accepted fact/rumor in Panama is that most of the condos—in fact, most of the bigger construction projects in the '80s and '90s—were financed by drug proceeds.

I was at a speaking engagement on money laundering at one of the major hotels in Panama City a couple of years ago. During the speech, I was trying to explain how a commercial real estate transaction could be used to conceal and launder money. As an example, I asked them to imagine someone trying to use drug money to purchase the hotel we were in. When I said the words "this hotel," the entire room erupted into laughter. The joke, I later learned, was that someone *had* purchased that hotel using drug money, or so it was rumored. I was disappointed to hear it. I just thought my delivery was improving.

Hold the Pepperoni

The effect of organized crime on society usually shows up in things like increased public corruption, higher availability of drugs and the like. But occasionally, it can affect daily life in ways that you would never have imagined. Some pages back, I listed a number of them. Here's another one that pertains to Canada, Montreal specifically; and it has to do with pizza, of all things.

Pizza is one of the most popular foods in North America and the pizza business generates billions of dollars each year for retailers, franchisers and food wholesalers. Aside from the exotic varieties, the recipe for traditional pizza is pretty consistent everywhere. Go into any restaurant in North America and order a pepperoni pizza and you won't be surprised at what you get. A crust on the bottom, covered with sauce, then cheese and, finally, twenty to thirty thin, half-dollar-sized slices of cooked pepperoni spread out on top.

But in Montreal, they like it different. In Montreal, the construction is like this: crust, sauce, and then about a hundred pieces of uncooked pepperoni, concealed under tons of cheese. Gross? Well, maybe to you and me, but in Montreal they'll send it back if it isn't made like that.

OK. So what?

In the early 1970s, Italian organized crime virtually controlled the pizza supply business in Montreal, particularly in the city's east end. The pizza supply "sales representatives" would come to a small mom-and-pop pizza parlor and say, "From the size of this joint, we estimate that you'll need 100 pounds of pepperoni and 200 pounds of mozzarella every week." Mom and Pop would typically only need about a quarter of that for the amount of business they were doing, but these guys weren't making a suggestion. Mom and Pop were being extorted. So what did they do? They bought those quantities of meat and cheese, of course.

So now that they are getting all this extra pepperoni and mozzarella every week, what are they going to do with it? Put it on the pizzas, of course. And that's exactly what they did, and so did all of the other Moms and Pops in the east end. They would throw all the extra pepperoni on the pizzas and then hide it under a thick layer of the extra mozzarella they were forced to buy. This went on for so long that people got used to it and it became the status quo.

The mob doesn't control the pizza supply business in Montreal anymore, but the pizza makers are still making pizzas that way.

Dopers I Have Known

George Howard Maxwell (this is one of the names that I changed) is a rather boring name for a drug smuggler. It doesn't really roll off the tongue like "Escobar," but in dope circles, he was no slouch. U.S. Customs had wanted a piece of his ass for years and had spent no small amount of time and money trying to take him out. Maxwell had made, and spent, a veritable

> An open foe may prove a curse,
> But a pretended friend is worse.
> *Fables (1727)*
> JOHN GAY
> *(1685–1732)*

fortune over his twenty years in the trade, smuggling marijuana and cocaine into south Florida.

Years earlier, one of Maxwell's ships was being pursued by U.S. Customs and the Coast Guard, so he scuttled it, dope and all. It sank in the Caribbean with his multi-ton load of marijuana on board. Neither Customs nor the DEA (the U.S. Drug Enforcement Agency) had ever been able to make a case against him. They knew his money was all from drug sales, but they couldn't prove it.

U.S. Customs found out that Maxwell was planning to wire-transfer some money out of one of his Swiss accounts to purchase a million dollars worth of gold coins from the Toronto office of a well-known foreign exchange dealer. The exchange was run as a pretty sophisticated organization and there's no way that they would ever have allowed the transaction to take place, but they were also good corporate citizens: they agreed to assist the United States government. So we came up with a plan.

My partner in this operation was Brian Abrams. Brian is probably the best undercover operator I ever worked with. Talk about an overachiever; this guy is a Golden Gloves boxer, a rodeo rider, a professional musician and singer whose band has released a couple of CDs. He's also a Junior "A" hockey player who was drafted by the pros, a husband and the father of two sons. And as if that wasn't enough, he got tired of being a cop, so he quit, went to law school, became a lawyer, joined a law firm and made partner in about two years. Up against Brian, Maxwell was in trouble. Brian went over to the foreign exchange house and posed as an employee. U.S. Customs' intelligence, as usual, was very good. At the predicted time, Maxwell called and spoke to Brian. Brian spun him around pretty good over the next day or two and gathered a lot of good information. Maxwell, in spite of never being convicted, had serious

> It is double the pleasure to deceive the deceiver.
>
> JEAN DE LA FONTAINE
> (1621–95)

money troubles, as well as personal ones. His son, who had been living in Colorado, had recently committed suicide. Then the government, I think it was the IRS, seized his property in Florida and Colorado. We later found out that, except for a few hundred thousand in cash, this $1 million in Switzerland was all the money Maxwell had left.

Maxwell had some kind of Native connection through his wife. He was hiding out on the Kahnewake Indian Reserve near Montreal. For that reason, he asked us to purchase a million dollars worth of gold Maple Leaf coins and have them shipped by armored car to a credit union on the reserve. He felt fairly secure there, because law enforcement agents are reluctant to undertake any kind of police action on Native land. On most reserves in North America, particularly those on the borders, there are Native organized crime groups that are involved in smuggling contraband, usually cigarettes and liquor, but sometimes narcotics and aliens as well. These organized crime groups intimidate and manipulate the rest of the Natives on the reserve, who are just regular people trying to get through their day like everyone else. The groups have become quite adept at manipulating the media as well, turning every attempt at interdicting their criminal activities into some kind of Native rights issue. They have successfully bamboozled the U.S. and Canadian governments into allowing them to operate with impunity. The politicians are afraid that if they make a move against Native organized crime, they might lose the votes of unenlightened "soccer moms" who believe everything they read in the paper.

When Maxwell called from the reserve, Brian could tell, even over the phone, that the guy was teetering on the edge, psychologically. In spite of being this big international drug smuggler, he was clearly going through a pretty rough patch and needed a friend. It was Brian's chance to manipulate him. They made an agreement, and Maxwell sent the money for the gold coins. Our guys seized it, of course. When Maxwell called to ask if it got there OK, Brian told him that he (Brian) was in big trouble with his employer. Not only had the cops frozen the $1 million, but he'd done the deal on Maxwell's say-so and now his employer was left holding the bag on the equivalent in gold Maple Leafs. He told Maxwell that the service charges alone were going to get him fired.

Maxwell was beside himself. Never doubting that Brian was his friend, he asked what could be done. "Can't you just send the money back to Switzerland?" Not when the government had frozen it, Brian explained. Then, dropping his voice conspiratorially, he told Maxwell that his cousin, Chris, was probably the only person who could help him out. Chris had done something like this before for another guy, he said. He'd gone to the government, told them that the other guy's money was in fact his, and it had worked out. The government had given the money back. Maxwell went for it.

A meeting was set up between Brian, Maxwell and me. Maxwell left the Indian reserve and drove to Toronto. He met us at the undercover offices of Inter-Cay Financial Investments. Before meeting with me, Brian began to work Maxwell hard, trying to get him off balance so he would be more pliable when he met me. The whole goal of the exercise was to get Maxwell to say out loud that the million was the proceeds of drug sales. We already had his money; we wanted to make sure that we got to keep it. Besides, Special Agent Terry Neeley, the U.S. Customs attaché at the embassy in Ottawa who had put the whole thing together, was one of my closest friends. We didn't want to let him down. Customs had sent us many good cases over the years, so we felt that we owed them this one.

Brian had warned Maxwell to be straight with me, but he started lying before I even had a chance to sit down. He was carrying some lame stock certificates for some oil-burner manufacturing company and tried to tell us that his money came from the sale of stock in a company that he owned. I searched my memory banks for some line that would work on this guy, since Brian already had his head spinning. I decided on a modified Godfather routine, countering with something stupid very much like, "How can you lie to me on my daughter's wedding day?" Hey, don't laugh. It worked.

What I really told Maxwell was that if he was going to lie, he might as well leave. I told him that I didn't care if the money was drug money, but I needed to know. If it was, I said, I would have to do a bunch of extra things to conceal its source.

> I hope that you have not been leading a double life, pretending to be wicked and being really good all the time. That would be hypocrisy.
>
> *The Importance of Being Earnest (1895)*
> OSCAR WILDE
> *(1854–1900)*

We were really pouring it on, pretending to be gangsters. Over the years, I've found that the crooks' perception of their own world is also shaped by popular culture. We could say things to them that were straight out of films, and they'd be impressed. There's a very curious psychology to the whole thing. At first, when we watched the tapes of meetings afterwards, we felt foolish, but we eventually figured out that this was what many of them wanted to hear.

Then all of a sudden Maxwell started confessing to everything: how he's a big drug smuggler, how he made millions doing it, how if this thing doesn't work, he's going to buy a boat, take off to Belize and hide out. We acted sympathetic and told him we'll try to fix the problem.

Then, right after the meeting, he disappeared. For a couple of months, we heard nothing. Turned out he had gone to Florida and bought a boat. He hired a captain to sail the boat to Belize. Coincidentally, the captain of the boat had two jobs; he was also an informant for U.S. Customs. Customs hit the boat before it sailed and caught Maxwell and his wife with a kilo of cocaine.

When a prosecutor and one of our investigators went to interview Maxwell in jail, he was in pretty bad shape. First of all, our gangster act must have worked even better than we thought, because he refused to give them any information about Brian and me. Then he spilled enough information on scuttling the boat with the marijuana load that Customs were able to send divers down and find it.

If you still think the life of an international drug trafficker is potentially exciting, the epilogue of this story will dispel that once and for all. After they got pinched, Maxwell and his wife were at some kind of co-ed jail where the men and the women were just separated by a fence. He told the investigator that his wife was having an affair with another male inmate. When the investigator asked how they were "getting together," Maxwell replied, "through the fence."

I imagine he's still in prison.

The Russians Are Coming

In the last years of the Soviet Union, the KGB found themselves in a bit of a cash crunch. Running an offensive intelligence service takes copious quantities of cash, and I don't mean rubles. It takes real money—American dollars—and the fact was, they didn't have any. So the KGB reached out to its operatives around the world and told them that they would now be responsible for financing their own operations. The irony of having to resort to capitalism to support a Communist regime was not lost on the field operatives, but since the U.S. dollar is the international currency of crime, and most of their informants and spies were criminals anyway, they quickly got into the business of selling drugs and shipping arms, with sidelines in blackmail and extortion.

When the USSR finally crashed, many of the agents and almost all of the people working in their networks found themselves out of a job. What were they to do? Well, continue to commit crimes, of course. But now they got to keep the money.

The result was a sophisticated network of professional criminals, which has spread out around the world. Many of these criminals left the former USSR, usually via Israel, and established themselves in Europe and North America, where they have had great success. Imagine, if you will, just for a moment, criminal groups that had flourished in the U.S.S.R., one of the most oppressive political regimes in history. What do you think happens when they get into a democratic society?

I was involved in a deal once with some Russian bad guys. While all of our people are waiting for them to show up with the dope, they decide to stop along the way and break into a couple of private homes so they could steal a couple of TVs and maybe a VCR. They ended up getting pinched by some uniformed cops, who discovered a million dollars worth of dope in the trunk of their car. For the life of me, I couldn't figure it out until a Russian cop told me, "To these guys, your country is just like a mall." In a city where every house is like a showroom of valuable consumer goods, I guess they couldn't resist a little "light stealing."

Many of these guys are former soldiers, veterans of the Afghanistan conflict. They are hard people, and they scare the shit out of our domestic bad guys. In the early '90s, after a shootout in Toronto between two Russian gangs, some cops I know brought a few of the participants back to the station for a photo opportunity. The arrested men were strip-searched, and it was discovered that one of them had a bullet wound to the thigh—but not from the shootout. The wound appeared to be about two weeks old, and the Russian guy had simply put a field dressing on it and kept going. It obviously didn't slow him down that much, as he was able to take part in another gun battle. Anyway, when the cops suggested a trip to emergency to have it treated, he told them that it was unnecessary, since the injury was what's known in the trade as a "through and through" wound. The bullet had come out the back and had not struck any bone or arteries.

These guys are hard. If that had been me, I'd still be whining about it.

So after all those years of the Cold War, our worst nightmare has finally come true; we've been invaded by the Russians.

A Formula for Success: (YBM + RTO + TSE) = FBI

Throughout the 1990s, Russian organized crime was flourishing inside the former USSR, too. The most successful of the organized crime groups was the infamous Solnetskaya gang. One of their top guys, Semion Yukovich Mogilevich, moved $15 billion through the Bank of New York in six months.[10] Mogilevich is a well-known international criminal, reputedly involved in extortion, prostitution, arms dealing and drug trafficking. In the mid-'90s, with the help of a lawyer, he was laundering money through a bank in London. When the U.K. authorities shut down his operation there, he needed to find a new place to play. He chose North America.[11]

If there's one thing that serious crooks are good at, it's planning ahead. Guys like Mogilevich have more backup systems than the space shuttle. For example, before he was even kicked out of Britain for money laundering in 1995, Mogilevich began a stock scam in Canada and the U.S., using Arigon, a Channel Islands corporation that he had established in 1991.

With Arigon, he effected a reverse takeover (RTO) of a company that eventually became known as YBM Magnex. The company, based in Newton, Pennsylvania, began trading on the Toronto Stock Exchange (TSE), Canada's most prestigious exchange.

The board of directors of YBM read like a Who's Who of

Canadian business people. It even included a former premier of the province of Ontario. Spurred on by an ever-increasing cash flow and sales figures that doubled in two years, YBM was the darling of the market. Everybody wanted in. Securities firms and pension funds took huge positions in the stock and watched it climb from $5 to $20 a share. The U.S. Attorney would eventually describe the YBM annual report as ranking "among the great works of modern fiction."[12]

YBM was supposedly producing magnets and bicycles, with facilities in Pennsylvania and Hungary. In reality, they were producing nothing. It was a complete contrivance, established by Mogilevich to launder the proceeds of his criminal activities in eastern Europe. All the transactions that the company reported were fake. No real business ever took place. Companies represented in the records and tax returns as customers of YBM in fact never were. Most of them didn't even exist. One of those false customers was a small New York company known as Benex. Remember that name—it's important.

Rumors started to spread about organized crime involvement. There was plenty of information available about who Mogilevich was, and it was known that he was one of the original shareholders. One of the directors even testified at a hearing before securities regulators that he had been visited by the FBI in April 1996 and told that there was organized crime involvement in YBM.[13]

On May 13, 1998, the FBI, U.S. Customs and the IRS raided the YBM offices in Pennsylvania and carted away thousands of pages of documents. YBM stock was suspended from trading on the TSE.

The members of the board of directors had prided themselves on being sophisticated businessmen, "big shooters," as they like to call themselves, in the concrete jungle that is the financial district; but in Mogilevich's jungle, they were just food. In the end, the directors lost their reputations, the investors lost $150 million, and Mogilevich didn't lose anything. In fact, he made $18 million and his three co-conspirators together made about the same.[14]

The Bank of New York

Beating taxes, duties and foreign exchange controls is the national sport in Russia. No one wants to tithe money off to a government that redefines corruption on an almost daily basis. There was an obvious opportunity there for someone with the right connections, no conscience and the ability to move money internationally. Lucy Edwards was that someone.

The Russian-born Edwards was an executive at the Bank of New York. Between February 1996 and July 1999, Edwards and her husband, Peter Berlin, through a company known as Benex that they established, successfully laundered almost $7 billion for Russian industrialists, politicians and criminals. The indictment against them stated that "bank accounts created by the defendants were used to promote a scheme to evade Russian currency control regulations and to conceal commissions illegally generated by the scheme offshore."[15]

Edwards and Berlin set up numerous accounts on behalf of shell corporations. To conceal their activities, they counted on the huge traffic of wire transfers, almost a trillion dollars a day, that constantly go through banks in New York City. But in August of 1999, the scheme began to unravel. The Republic National Bank, using special software designed to monitor correspondent bank wire transfers, detected suspicious transactions relating to Edwards and Berlin's companies. An investigator from Republic drove out to the address in Queens, New York, that Benex had provided. Not surprisingly, Benex didn't have any offices there.[16] Republic called the regulators. The regulators called the FBI. The FBI arrested Edwards and Berlin and got them rooms at the Crowbar Hotel.*

Edwards and Berlin pleaded guilty in 2000 to two counts of money laundering on a plea bargain in return for their

* Jail

"assistance."[17] Edwards admitted to allowing Russian bankers, who were complicit in the scheme, to use the Bank of New York's electronic banking software to transfer money for their Russian clients.

Their take? A meager $1.8 million. Not really a whole lot of money to get in exchange for your soul.

In the end, the Bank of New York suffered a huge loss of reputation. The bank's CEO, Thomas Renyi, testifying in front of the House Banking Committee, referred to his own bank as "the poster child for money laundering." He admitted that the whole affair was due to a "lapse" on the part of the bank.[18] (Sorry, Tom, for the rest of us, a lapse is more like leaving the milk out on the kitchen counter overnight, not allowing Russian gangsters to launder billions of dollars through your bank.)

In April 2003, long after the YBM affair and the Bank of New York guilty pleas, the U.S. Attorney's office finally prepared indictments against Mogilevich and the others on forty-five separate counts of everything from RICO violations (offenses under the Racketeer Influenced and Corrupt Organizations Act) to wire fraud. The substance of the indictment was that "the defendants inflated the value of YBM stock so they could profit at the public's expense. Books were cooked, auditors were deceived, bribes were offered to accountants."

Just how bad are these guys? The answer to that question is: really bad. In 1998, a reporter from *The Village Voice* wrote an article on Mogilevich, exposing his criminal activities. Shortly after that, the CIA picked up information off a wiretap that Mogilevich planned to have the reporter killed.[19] (The reporter went into hiding for several months.) And when Mogilevich's associate, Sergei Mikhailov, was indicted by the Swiss on money laundering charges, the Solnetskaya gang's response was a simple one. They threatened the Swiss government. They told them that if Mikhailov wasn't released and they didn't stop prosecuting the gang, they would blow up the Swiss embassy in Moscow. The Swiss took them seriously and spent millions upgrading security at the embassy.[20]

Eventually, the charges against Mikhailov were dropped, for whatever reason, and Carla del Ponte, the prosecutor who made the first cases against the Russians and the Swiss banks, left the case when she was promoted to the UN War Crimes Tribunal in The Hague.[21]

Mogilevich is still out there somewhere—probably working a new scam.

Should It Be Legal?

Very few people grow their own marijuana. It takes time, skill, patience and lots of expensive equipment to be able to produce a marijuana plant with sufficient THC to get someone properly high. So most people buy it. And they pay whatever the dealers ask.

Wherever there's easy money to be made, bad guys will be found. Lately, the most popular, and potent, marijuana is grown on the west coast of Canada. Marijuana production in the province of British Columbia recently surpassed lumber and tourism in revenue. But if you think that it might be a good idea to move out there and start your own grow operation, think again. The whole industry is controlled by organized crime; specifically, Asian gangs and outlaw motorcycle gangs. If you start growing marijuana out there and selling it, before too long they will pay you a call. They will tell you that you can grow it and sell it as long as you only sell it to them, at the price that they set. This is a cartel—just like the ones that everyone has heard about in

> Doctors smoke it
> Nurses smoke it
> Judges smoke it
> Even the lawyers too
> Legalize it
> That's the best thing you can do
> *"Legalize It"* (1976)
> *CBS Records*
> Peter Tosh
> *(1944–87)*

"There's one really important reason why marijuana should be legalized...

...What was that reason again?

ANONYMOUS

the Colombian cocaine trade.

Drug trafficking is the biggest illegal industry in the world and is often the preferred source of funds for violent terrorist groups, too. For many, the logical solution to the problem is to legalize drug use. Politicians in a number of so-called enlightened countries have recently started to make a case for the legalization of marijuana. Those who support the decriminalization of drugs say that normally law-abiding citizens are being persecuted for their use of a supposedly harmless drug. They often use the prohibition of alcohol from 1920 to 1933 in the U.S. to support their position, arguing that it created a whole new class of criminals, bootleggers and rumrunners.

Their idea is that government should step in, regulate the sale of marijuana and apply a tax to it. Imagine the bureaucracy! Governments are the only people in the world who could sell drugs and still lose money at it!!

And let's not forget the very vocal minority that support the use of "medicinal marijuana" to treat everything from lung cancer to athlete's foot. For them, it's a human rights thing. I say, if the supporters of medicinal marijuana—most of whom, coincidentally, seem to resemble Grateful Dead fans—find that smoking grass eases their pain, why not let them?

I still think it's baloney, though. There are plenty of legal analgesic substances out there that I'm sure are far more effective at reducing discomfort than the evil weed. Not to forget the fact that the whole idea of using smoking as a delivery method for a drug seems pretty stupid in the first place.

But I'm sure that twenty-five years from now, when we're all using neuro-stimulators to get high, people will think this whole debate was childish. That is, if they're still able to think.

There's no doubt that the prohibition against alcohol permanently installed Italian organized crime in American society, but that doesn't mean that legalizing drugs would make organized crime disappear. Whether or not marijuana is harmless is up to the scientists to prove. But if you want to see why legalizing marijuana is such a dumb idea, go to Amsterdam. Although the Dutch police still interdict the flow of cannabis drugs that are transshipped through the Netherlands, they have a "hands off" approach to domestic consumption. As a result, every doper in Europe seems to have relocated there. The streets are full of a lot of people who seem to be doing nothing more than hanging around. It's tough to support the idea that marijuana use leads to stronger drugs, but perhaps because of the permissiveness, there are a lot of heroin addicts there as well. At least, it seems that way from the number of used syringes you see littering the parks and alleys. If our governments decided to legalize the stuff, the world would be one big Amsterdam.

If you've spent your life fighting it, it's hard to be objective about drugs. Although many people can still lead a fairly productive life while being high most of the time, there's a whole segment of society that can't. This is the usually the same segment of society that also has a hard time keeping a job and not beating their kids.

Without being too dogmatic about it, the truth is, some people need to be protected from their own weaknesses and that's why we should never stop the fight against drugs. The trick is to fight the war on both fronts: in source countries where they produce it and here in our own country, where the demand is.

A Day in the Life of the Drug Trade

The mechanics of laundering drug money will be clearer if I give you a detailed example. Let's start with some small-time crooks.

Street drug dealers usually don't have much trouble dealing with the cash that they generate. If Junior, a local crack dealer, makes $2,000 a week, all he has to do is pay for things like rent, groceries, etc., in cash. If he has a bank account, chances are the bank wouldn't say much even if Junior deposited the whole $2,000 in cash every week. The problems start when you make $20,000 or $200,000 a week. And there's plenty of guys that do! So what do they do to get rid of their money? Before I can explain that, you have to understand how drug trafficking works.

Most large drug importations operate on a mixture of cash and credit. It's actually an amazing system of trade finance, because they function without letters of credit and often without using the international banking system. It's based primarily on trust. That and the fact that if there's a dispute, chances are you'll be murdered. The fear factor keeps everybody relatively honest, too.

As an example, let's consider a drug trafficking organization based in Guyana. The guy at the top of this organization—we'll call him Desmond—has people all over the world who import his cocaine into their countries. Logistically, it's a complex undertaking. Issues such as transportation, finance, security and communications, just to name a few, all have to be controlled and coordinated. On a regular basis, Desmond's agents move cocaine to North America and Europe. So let's say on January 1, a shipment of cocaine arrives in Houston. It is broken up into smaller lots by the members of the organization and distributed to the other representatives. Let's call them Jack, Moe and Manny in New York, Detroit and Toronto. From there, some might go to a lab to be converted into crack cocaine. (Crack cocaine was invented by Dominicans. Apart from supplying most of the better players in major-league baseball, this appears to be their only noteworthy contribution to society.) But whether it's rock or powder, it's then sold to other organizations. And so on and so on, right down to small-time dealers like Junior.

Guys like Junior usually take their dope "on the cuff"—on credit.

They don't have to pay for it right away. Also known as a "front." The term "on the cuff" dates back to the days when men wore shirts that had detachable collars and cuffs. When someone bought merchandise and promised to pay later, the merchant would often make a note of the transaction on his shirt cuff and save it as a record.

So Junior takes the drugs and, at the end of a prearranged time period, he pays, and the money goes back up the ladder with all the other dealers' money. It all goes to Manny, the main distributor in Junior's city. Manny also got his drugs on the cuff, so now that he has the cash, he reaches out for Desmond, letting him know he has, say $2 million, in cash, ready for delivery to him. Desmond tells Manny that he'll call him back with the details on what he should do with it.

Desmond then puts the word out to a variety of groups around North America, saying that he has $2 million in Toronto that he needs to have picked up and sent to him. The money doesn't all go back to Guyana, though. Around $1 million goes to his supplier in Venezuela. Another $400,000 goes to the guys who actually physically moved the dope. From the $600,000 that is left, Desmond will pay a few other people and also somewhere between $150,000 and $250,000 to the people who picked up the money and moved it. The remaining money is his profit.

There are various organizations around the world that will pick up drug money and, for a substantial fee, convert it into some other monetary instrument or wire-transfer it to wherever you want. Those are the people Desmond is now calling on. After a day or two, he gets offers from a number of money brokers who are able to move the money to the various places where he wants it. One group, for example, might say that they can do it within five business days for 10 percent of the principal, that is, $200,000. Another group might offer to do it faster but for a bit more money. Desmond's choice is based on a number of factors. He may have done business with them before; he may owe people money and need to get it to them right away; he may need the money to finance another shipment.

Desmond also knows that any one of those money-brokering groups might turn out to be cops. From time to time the police, using informers and undercover agents, will establish "front" businesses, like we did, and then become one of the groups vying for the business. The purpose, as I've mentioned, was to gather evidence of the "substantive offense," usually drug trafficking. You see, without the substantive offense, there's no crime. Money laundering isn't money laundering without a criminal act. You don't ever see anyone indicted for just the offense of money laundering; there's always another offense to go with it. And it can't just be any offense: the person has to be dealing with the proceeds of a "designated offense." In most countries, this is pretty well any serious crime. In other countries, the designation is less all-encompassing. For example, in Trinidad, money laundering isn't money laundering unless the source of the money is drug trafficking.

Even if Desmond has been tipped off that a certain group is probably a police front, he may decide to move the money through them anyway. Once in a while, big drug organizations will make use of a police "sting" operation even though they are pretty sure it's the police. They know that if they give money to the police to be wire-transferred to some far-off land, it will get there, unless the police decide to seize it, which is a risk the bad guys may be prepared to take. They obviously won't do it more than once, because the more times they do it, the more evidence the police will have. The bad guys will use that if it's to their advantage.

When I operated businesses of this kind during the 1980s and '90s, the main thing we were always worried about (besides getting shot) was that we might be facilitating criminal activity. The rule of thumb was that for every dollar we "laundered," we should seize four dollars at the end of the operation.

I once had a serious argument with some local cops in Canada over this exact issue. These guys were investigating the Colombians, and they had wiretaps on absolutely everybody. They knew that the Colombians were about to smuggle several million dollars in cash back down to South America, but they were going to let it go so they could make a huge bust when the next shipment came up. These guys were honest, hardworking investigators and they were hugely dedicated. My point to them was that they should just arrest everyone right away for conspiracy and seize the money. They didn't want to, for a couple of reasons.

First, they didn't want a "dry" conspiracy. This is what happens when the bad guys are all arrested but no narcotics are seized. This type of case is harder to prove because the police have to rely on the bad guys' telephone conversations and convict them solely on the evidence of their *intent* to import the drugs. Dry conspiracies usually result when an operation has to be called off because continuing it would threaten the safety of an undercover operator or an informant. Their second objection was that their police department wouldn't get to keep the money.* My response to them was that they didn't get to keep the dope either! In the end, they did the right thing and a lot of traffickers got locked up.

So Desmond, back in Guyana, has to think about all these factors when he chooses a group to move his money. Once he's done that, the brokers will supply him with a mobile phone, a pager number or an email address. Desmond provides this information to Manny, his representative in Toronto, usually by email. He tells Manny to follow the money brokers' instructions.

---

* It's different now in Canada. The police force doesn't get to keep the money, but the provincial government does; it is supposed to result in the police getting a higher budget if they seize lots of drug money. In reality, I don't think that much of the money ever trickles down to the police to pay for salaries, overtime, etc.

Manny contacts the money guys directly and they give him instructions. More than likely, they will tell him to go to a parking lot at a specific time, and place his money in the unlocked trunk of a car. This kind of thing is pretty risky and is also fraught with the possibility of double crosses. A bunch of really bad things could happen. The money people could meet Manny, murder him, take the money and tell Desmond that he never showed up. Other bad guys, aware that Manny is a dealer, could be watching him and then rip him off. The cops could be on to Manny and planning to arrest him—and they'd take the money, too. After which he would still owe it to Desmond. All of you budding dope dealers out there should be aware that the police are considered just another one of the risks of doing business, and if you lose the cash, the dope or both, that's your problem. No matter what happens, the people you are doing business with will still expect to get paid.

Most of the time, though, the bad guys get their money delivered where they want it, when they want it. Deals in the underworld don't go sour nearly as often as they do in the private sector, that is, the "legitimate" business world. In the criminal world, nobody gets sued and no one ever gets a snotty letter from a lawyer. If things get screwed up, they just kill you. At the end of the day, it's a much more efficient system and it's based on trust—and fear, of course.

All of these transactions are in American dollars, and for dealers like Manny, who aren't in the U.S., this presents an additional problem. The money they collect is all in their local currency. In the international drug trade, non-U.S. currencies are pretty much worthless outside their own countries; even Deutschmarks or sterling, which are normally widely accepted around the world in international business, will sometimes be refused by criminals. Central banks in most countries track the international flow of their currencies. (The United States tracks its money around the world and also through the U.S. itself; this is done by the U.S. Office of the Comptroller of

Currency [OCC].) If large amounts of a particular currency begin to flow back to a given country from a location like Colombia, it's pretty obvious that there's something fishy going on. That type of "heat" causes problems. During the 1970s and '80s, the U.S. Federal Reserve noted that inordinately large amounts of cash were being generated in the Miami area as a direct result of the drug trade.

People commit crimes to make money so they can get power and so they can buy stuff. But, in most cases, they need to pay for things in their own currency. If you're doing a legitimate business deal, the bank will convert your money for you. You give dollars to a U.S. bank, they wire-transfer it to Bogotá, and when the person picks it up at the other end, he or she receives it in pesos (less the commission and government tariff). But Colombian criminals need pesos, and they can't convert their U.S. dollars into pesos in the ordinary way.

The Colombian traffickers were faced with a huge problem during the late 1980s and early 1990s. They had huge amounts of U.S. cash and they didn't know how to get rid of it. They had it stashed in the U.S. and in Colombia. Pablo Escobar went so far as to construct a huge, glass-lined barn, just to store currency. The reason that it was glass-lined was that rats had been burrowing in and eating the cash.

Avi and Albert's Boiler Room

One of the most popular and successful schemes is the classic boiler-room fraud. These scams began with the advent of the telephone and still continue. The name apparently comes from the old days when these operations were hidden in the basements, quite often literally the boiler rooms of buildings

My father must have had some elementary education for he could read and write and keep accounts inaccurately.
GEORGE BERNARD SHAW
(1856–1950)

A boiler-room operation is an office from which potential customers are called by high-pressure salesmen who attempt to sell stocks.
Many low-end brokerage houses employ this technique to push a particular stock that they wish to promote. The danger, of course, is that
those promoting the stock may also be holding a substantial position in
it. On the street, this is referred to as a "pump and dump" scheme. The
essence of the pump and dump is that the price of a stock is artificially
inflated by hype and promotion, and then, once those promoting it
have "pumped" the price up high enough, they "dump" their stock at
the inflated price and leave everybody else holding the bag.

Some boiler-room operations may not even be illegal; they can
also be legitimate telemarketing enterprises. These are the guys who
call your house when you're having dinner and try to sell you carpet
cleaning or new windows. The boiler-room aspect is just the technique. Organized criminal groups have used the boiler-room
approach successfully to flog worthless metals, stamps and gems, as
well as stocks. Historically, these groups operated from several cen-
ters in North America. These were:

Lake Havesu, Arizona
Orange County, California
Montreal, Quebec
Boca Raton, Florida
Toronto, Ontario

For some reason, local conditions in these places were conducive
to the type of setup that the crooks needed to make these scams work.

The first requirement was a local phone company that didn't
mind installing a whole bunch of telephones in one little office; of
course, mobile phones have changed the face of this crime because
now you can do it from anywhere.

Another advantage was a police force that wasn't very interested
in this kind of crime. The crooks always took advantage of any juris-

dictional compartmentalization to thwart law enforcement. Typically, they would operate a boiler room in one country, say Canada, for example, which would only target U.S. victims. Then they would use a bank in a third country, such as the Bahamas, to deposit the proceeds. The bad guys knew how difficult it was for the police to investigate their activities if they were stretched across multiple jurisdictions. So for many years, these guys operated pretty much in the clear.

All boiler-room operations work off what's known as a "sucker list." This is exactly what it sounds like: a list of suckers who will easily fall for a scam. These lists are very valuable and are bought and sold by criminal groups all over the U.S. and Canada. The people on these lists are usually older; often they are quite elderly.

Some years ago, the FBI was successful in having the names of some retired FBI agents placed on these sucker lists. The U.S. and Canadian governments decided to work together and put some of these groups down. A fund was established so the victims would be able to get their money back after the cops were finished their investigation.

That's where I came in. My "money laundering" colleagues and I became involved with two Russian Israeli brothers, Avi and Albert, who were running a precious-metal scam and targeting mostly elderly victims. I was buying the checks they received from the victims for 70 to 80 cents on the dollar. Buyers of third-party checks are often money launderers. A third-party check is simply a check that is not made out to you but has been endorsed by the payee. Once endorsed, it can be bought and sold like anything else.

Avi and Albert were in my office one day telling me how they had ripped off some poor old guy for ten or fifteen thousand bucks. They were laughing because the victim had been so excited about his investment. He had told them that he wanted to pay for his grandson's education, and they had convinced him that he would get enough from this deal to pay for it completely. To sit and watch these guys taking real pleasure from this is an experience every judge on the bench should have. It would give them a different take on the criminal mind. These guys were despicable; they were greedily ripping off innocent elderly victims, many of whom I suspect were senile. The writing on some of the checks was so feeble, so shaky, you could hardly make it out. Since I was laundering most of their proceeds, I was pretty much in on the whole scam. What amazed me about these guys was their grasp of the psychology of human behavior. They were experts at figuring out, in a very short time, what motivated their victims and then using that to con them.

One day, Avi told me that he was sending a victim back the $10,000 that they had conned out of him only weeks before. He said that the guy had called and explained that his wife had been diagnosed with cancer and he needed the money for medical expenses. This was surprising news. I asked Avi if he'd had some type of religious experience lately that had turned him from the low-life scumbag that he was into Israel's answer to Mother Teresa. His answer was very illuminating. To Avi, it was a simple business decision. Because of all the publicity around scams like theirs, what they needed at that time were solid, believable references from real citizens. Avi said they would get lots of mileage out of this by referring skeptical potential victims to the "$10,000 man," who would go on at great lengths about how great they were.

In the end, most of the victims got their money back, the world kept turning, and Avi and Albert went to jail. They got caught because, while I was posing as their money launderer, I was able to gather evidence of the substantive offense of fraud. They wouldn't have been able to commit these crimes without someone helping them launder the cash by buying the third-party checks. So who's helping crooks run scams like this? Mostly, criminals masquerading as legitimate business people.

The amazing thing about these scams is that the con men can

sometimes work the same victim two or three times. For example, if they were able to sell you four ounces of some obscure precious metal for $20,000 on their first pass, they will take another run at you and try to do you again. They will tell you that they have a potential buyer for your metal but that they are only dealing in eight-ounce lots, so you'll need to drop another $20,000 to bring your total up to an amount they can sell.

Another angle is to call victims and tell them that you represent a consumer group that is attempting to recover the funds from the initial fraudulent investment. Victims are solicited to contribute to a class action or some other type of legal baloney, and they end up getting fleeced one more time.

Gangster Schtick

Although bad guys usually conceal their true intentions and activities from those they wish to make use of, there are other times when it is their evil nature itself, and the aura of mystery and danger associated with it, that attracts people from the so-called straight world and draws them in. Of course, I happen to have an example of this.

> The devil hath power to assume a pleasing shape.
>
> *Hamlet*
> WILLIAM SHAKESPEARE
> *(1564–1616)*

In the early 1990s, I was operating a phony investment company for the government. It was a long-term undercover money operation targeting major international drug traffickers. We ran operations for law enforcement agencies from all over the world, setting up bank accounts and corporations for them and doing money pickups for the bad guys.

Crooks from all over the world came and went from my office daily, usually in the company of informants or other undercover

"Whenever you wish to do anything against the law, Cicely, always consult a good solicitor first."

Captain Brassbound's Conversion
GEORGE BERNARD SHAW
(1856–1950)

cops from a number of countries who made use of our setup to "backstop"[*] themselves.

Since there is no money laundering without the substantive criminal offense, my job and that of my colleagues was to gather the evidence of that substantive offense, which was usually drug trafficking. One investigation I participated in was named Project Once More. An informant introduced me to Raffel Christopher Sinclair, the leader of a Guyanese drug trafficking organization that was operating in Toronto and New York, importing cocaine from South America.

Chris Sinclair didn't want to be just a trafficker. His dream was to start a nightclub. He had found the perfect building, which was for sale at a price of $780,000. He wanted to buy it, but the money was a problem. Not that he didn't have any. He had tons. The problem was that it was all in cash.

So that's where I came in. Believing me to be a gangster and a money launderer, he asked me to help put the deal together. Chris's real estate agent friend, Charles, had already submitted an offer to purchase to the owners. The offer included a deposit, in the amount of $25,000, in the form of a certified check from the trust account of Charles's real estate company. Chris had originally provided the deposit to Charles in cash, and Charles had subsequently deposited the money in the trust account. But that was about as far as he could go. Any more big cash deposits like that and Charles was going to "heat himself up."[**]

---

[*] "Backstopping" is the creation of a false history that makes people think your identity is that of a real individual.

[**] Attract the interest of the police.

I established a company for Chris that would act as the business front for his activities. We agreed that each of us would provide one person from our respective organizations to act as directors of the company in order to conceal Chris's involvement. Chris provided his friend Charles, the real estate agent. I provided my friend Umberto,* an undercover RCMP officer.

Umberto and I selected a lawyer from the telephone directory, at random, to complete the real estate transaction on our behalf. Then we called her up and went to see her at her office.

Before I take this story any further, you need to know a couple of things. We were pretending to be gangsters—Jewish/Sicilian gangsters, to be exact. I was the boss and all my friends were the gang. We drove Benzes and Caddies, wore tons of jewelry and had really expensive suits. I even went for manicures! We walked, talked and acted like gangsters. It was a hoot, especially for guys who, in reality, weren't earning much more than $70,000 a year. It was the ultimate game of cops and robbers—except that we were playing with real guns.

When we got to the lawyer's office, Umberto and I explained the nature of our proposed real estate transaction to her. She appeared very interested. In fact, Umberto and I both noticed something strange about her reaction to our appearance and demeanor. It was apparent that she found the idea of associating with gangsters appealing. At one point, she said to me, smiling, "You guys are in the Mafia." I gave her the usual answer, "There's no such thing as the Mafia. That's just in the movies." She then said, "Well, I think you guys are money launderers, anyway," which I of course denied.

I told her that the directors of the company we were in the process of establishing would be Umberto and our client's guy, Charles the real estate agent. After Umberto and I signed our part of

* Not his real name.

the documents, we told the lawyer that, since Charles wasn't with us, we'd take the papers to him and get a notary to witness his signature. Without any suggestion from us, she said, "I think I just saw him in the hallway. Why don't you take the papers out there and have him sign them?" Charles certainly wasn't out in the hallway. Besides, she didn't even know him.

What she was doing was counseling us to go out into the hallway, where we wouldn't be visible to her, forge Charles's signature on the documents and then return them to her. We didn't need to do that; we were prepared to do it legally. She had gotten caught up in the excitement of the moment, exhilarated by the thought that her colorful new clients were gangsters, and she was trying to give the impression that she was hip. It was pretty obvious that she wasn't.

A couple of days later, two of my "gang" went to see her again. They just wanted to make sure that Chris's real estate deal went smoothly. This time, she asked them what kind of business we were in. The boys told her that we were in the "asset protection" business. They told her that we utilized offshore structures to protect the assets of our clients. After listening to this, she made what she thought was a joke, referring to our clients, under her breath, as "criminals."

But by this point, she had totally bought into the whole gangster thing. She gave the boys unsolicited assurances that everything they said would be confidential. They said they had assumed that the client-solicitor privilege would extend to them as well. Her response was that we were her clients.

The purchase price was received, in cash, from the trafficker's money couriers, over the course of several days. We ultimately completed the transaction with this lawyer, paying $780,000 for a commercial building. The lady lawyer is, as far as I know, still practicing law by day and probably watching *The Sopranos* by night.

False Identification and Documentation

False identification is pretty easy to obtain. It is definitely not a function of your level of sophistication as a criminal; everybody on the street has phony ID. However, since most people in the straight world are completely unfamiliar with it, it's also a very easy thing for the bad guys to use. And notwithstanding all of the countermeasures that have been put into place since 9/11, in most countries you can still obtain false documents quite easily. You certainly don't have to go to all the trouble of counterfeiting it. You simply have to lie on your application form! In democratic countries, although we have plenty of rules, the whole setup is still basically an honor system. When you complete a passport application, most Western governments are satisfied that the small print under the signature box ("making a false statement is a criminal offense with a maximum penalty of blah, blah, blah…") is enough to keep people from committing a crime. If I was an international terrorist/criminal/drug dealer, I know it would scare the hell out of me.

> Fraud and deceit abound these days more than in former times.
> SIR EDWARD COKE
> *(1552–1634)*

> Criminal: A person with predatory instincts who has not sufficient capital to form a corporation.
> HOWARD SCOTT
> *(1926–)*

Go to any cemetery, find some kid who was born around the same time as you and died young. Apply for his or her birth certificate. Chances are you'll get it, because even now, with all the security scares, most jurisdictions still haven't married up the databases of birth and death certificates. Once you get the birth certificate, it's a relatively simple task to start applying for all the other pieces of identification that go along with it.

When I was a police officer, I must have signed a couple of dozen passport applications for friends and relatives, attesting that the photograph was a true likeness of the applicant, etc. I never once got a call from the Passport Office, asking me if the signature on the application was really mine or if the applicant was really who he said he was.

Some years ago, I was involved in a case where this lady decided that she was going to defraud the income tax department. At tax time, she went down to the tax office and asked for a stack of forms to give to the employees of the company where she supposedly worked. Then she filled out the appropriate income tax forms that showed that thirty or so people (all of them fictional) had been paid a substantial wage and that the necessary taxes had been deducted and remitted to the government. Then she completed tax returns for all of her alter egos and received a large refund.*

She was an eccentric old girl. When we finally arrested her, she was almost relieved. She had already established almost one hundred different identities, most of which had complete sets of identification and bank accounts to go along with them. I asked her how she kept track of everything and she told me that it was very difficult. Her biggest fear, it seems, was signing the wrong name when she went to the bank. She told me that she was in the habit of attaching a clothespin to her ear so the pain would keep her from forgetting what name she was using.

When we arrested her, she was in the process of applying for a whole new batch of identities. When the investigators went to the government office that issued birth certificates, they were actually in the process of mailing some of hers out to her. The person preparing the envelopes hadn't noticed that three birth certificates, in three different names, were being sent to the same post office box in the same small town. When investigators went to the office that issued

---

* I have intentionally left out a couple of very important steps in this scam, just in case some of you out there get the urge to give it a try.

the social security cards, they asked if it didn't seem strange to them that—since you need a social security number to have a job—they were getting so many applications from people who stated that they were in their thirties and forties.

> *Clerk:* So let me see now, sir, you're forty-eight years old and you are only now applying for a social security number?
> *Applicant:* Yeah, I was busy, you know…doing stuff. I just never got around to it.

They couldn't have all been living in a commune, eating brown rice and smoking pot for all these years.

Identity Theft and Other Misconceptions

Identity theft is a pretty big deal right now. You see stories in the news all the time about serious computer security breaches, where thousands of people have had their personal information lifted. In these stories, there are always quotes from so-called experts, usually consultants or government privacy nerds, about how the victims' credit histories might be affected forever. These people would have you believe that the bad guys who are out to steal your identity really want to *be* you, that is, assume your identity for an extended period of time. There are even companies out there that prey on people's anxiety about this and offer identity theft insurance.

For the most part, that's baloney. The truth is that identity theft, although it's real, is not the horrible threat to the consumer that these guys would have you believe. As with every issue, everybody has their own agenda and people will often exaggerate relatively minor risks just to scare you into voting for them, hiring them or buying their product.

The reality is the following: long-term identity theft is rare, although it does happen. In the case of money laundering, the person whose identity is being used will not suffer any loss (and therefore the fraud is far less likely to be detected and reported). If a money launderer establishes a bank account in your name, using a different address, and uses the account to warehouse drug proceeds, you would likely never know, since you wouldn't receive the bank statement. Even if you examined your credit history, you might not find any signs of your other life, depending on how (and if) the bank reported the account to the credit-reporting agency. It's hard to say how often this kind of thing happens because it's so difficult to detect.

Mostly, criminals who borrow your identity for motives of theft or fraud want to take as much as they can as fast as they can, not get caught, and move on to another victim. They don't want to "steal" your identity, they just want to borrow it for a while. The whole purpose of the exercise is to pretend they are you and obtain goods and/or services based on your ability to pay; i.e., your credit rating.

A lot of West African* organized crime groups are into this. Generally what they do is have one of their group, usually a woman, get a job at a place like a utility company or a mobile phone provider where she will have access to your personal information. Then they apply for a new credit card in your name and have it sent to another address. Or they just use your credit card number to order consumer goods over the Internet and have them delivered somewhere else.

---

* "West African" is a politically correct term for Nigerian. Political realities have forced law enforcement to drastically change their nomenclature. Russian organized crime is now Eastern European Organized Crime. Chinese and Vietnamese gangs are now Asian Organized Crime. One police department I knew of actually had a division, called the "Black Squad," that went after Caribbean crooks. The press went nuts over that one even though most of the cops on the squad were black. The cops didn't even bother changing the name; they just shut it down.

Now, this sounds simple, but in fact it isn't. First of all, the big credit-reporting companies have been in the business for years and have seen every possible scam. These companies have developed systems to flag certain addresses that they feel are associated with criminal activity. For example, if you apply for a credit card and you provide the address of some money remitter who has a bunch of mailboxes at his store that he rents to people by the month, it's going to be detected and you won't get the card. If a credit-reporting company receives a new application for credit from a cell phone retailer or a credit card company and the address supplied by the applicant is different from the one they have for that person, they will investigate it.

They do this for one simple reason. Even though it may cause some temporary confusion on your credit file, it's the cell phone and credit card companies, not you, who will be on the hook for any charges that the bad guys run up while they're using your name. So it's in these companies' best interests to check carefully before they send out a card, and they have developed all sorts of software to identify suspicious activity. They are able to detect changes in customer trends that may indicate fraud and/or identity theft with surprising efficiency. If you only use your card for gas and all of a sudden there's an airline ticket to Mogadishu charged to it, they're going to call you and ask what's happening. So if you're taking a trip to somewhere exotic or out of the ordinary, call your credit card provider and tell them. They will put a note in your file so you won't have any problems when you travel. Besides, when you're the victim of a sixty-minute kidnapping in Manila and the bad guys take you to the bank machine for the "ransom," this way, the transaction won't be refused and they might not kill you.

Because this credit card fraud is so rampant in e-commerce, most Internet retailers refuse to ship any goods purchased with a credit card unless the goods are being delivered to the billing address on the credit card. Retailers that do business with credit card companies are worried about "charge-backs." A charge-back occurs when a customer refuses to pay on the grounds that he or she did not receive the goods or services that were billed on his or her credit card account. This is a serious issue for retailers and service providers, as the charge-back rate can have an effect on the overall value of their business.

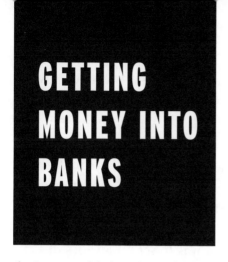

GETTING MONEY INTO BANKS

Nothing is worth doing unless the consequences may be serious.

GEORGE BERNARD SHAW
(1856–1950)

If fraud and theft are defined as getting money out of a company without the company finding out, then money laundering could be described as getting money into banks or companies without them finding out. Criminals have various techniques for accomplishing this.

Uri, I Hardly Knew Ya...

Gone are the days when you could just walk in off the street with a big bag of cash and make a deposit without anyone asking questions. The good guys are much more suspicious now. So what's a criminal to do? Well, you could always buy your own bank—but let's leave that for later. Another option is to make use of an employee. There are a couple of ways to do this. The first is to infiltrate the bank with your own people. If you don't think that organized crime groups have the foresight to place their people inside a bank, or any other corporation, for that matter, think again. They can do it, and they will continue to do it.

I know of a manufacturing company that fell victim to this kind of infiltration; they unwittingly hired four members of an organized crime group. These guys stole so much that they had to rent their own warehouse to store the swag.[*]

---

[*] Stolen merchandise.

But the best-laid plans can go wrong. When I was undercover, I met several times with a Russian mob guy named Uri Gitman. Foresight was only one of the talents that Uri and his colleagues possessed. They had placed one of their own people inside a Russian bank twenty years earlier. Their guy had done well, rising through the ranks and attaining a position of authority. Uri came to me and asked if I could help him move US$800 million that they planned to steal from the bank, using their inside man. Of course, I agreed to help. Anything to oblige. Their plan was to set up a series of fictitious transactions through front companies, using counterfeit letters of credit. Their confederate inside the bank was to make sure that the phony letters of credit were honored. However, the deal never took place, I'm sorry to say. It seems that Uri's foresight ran out. They found him in his apartment, the victim of what's known as a "Moscow suicide." He had shot himself in the head. Twice.

But I have to admit...I always thought his plan was good.

Blackmail and Extortion

When I was pretending to be a money launderer, the people whose money I looked after all assumed that I "had something" on somebody in a bank. That I knew somebody's secret that they

> Think how many blameless lives are brightened by the blazing indiscretions of other people.
> SAKI
> (1870–1916)

didn't want the rest of the world to know. Have you got any secrets like that? I know I do.

There are generally three ways to get people to do what you want. You can trick them, you can reward them, or you can threaten them. These are all quite effective, but in my experience, threatening works best. When you threaten violence, it's extortion, and when you threaten to expose a secret, it's blackmail: these have been favored tools of the criminal since men started walking upright. And the reason that these are such popular techniques is that they really work!

Spies—both on their side and ours—have used and continue to use a technique known as the "honey trap" to gather information. Crooks have been using it forever as well. But the bad guys who need to launder money are also able to use it. Suppose you're part of a drug trafficking organization, and your job is to find new ways to dispose of large volumes of cash. You can't get the cash into the bank without drawing suspicion. So what do you do? You find yourself a bank employee, someone who is high enough up on the corporate ladder that he or she will be able to help you out. Let's say it's a man: someone with kids, a wife, a house in the suburbs. From there, it's simply a matter of finding out which gym he goes to or which restaurants he frequents. Once you have him nailed down, you arrange for him to meet a woman.

For all of you ladies out there who believe that your husbands would say no, I hate to disappoint you, but the truth is, the woman the bad guys send will succeed. It doesn't matter who the guy is or how strong he is. That's just the way things work in the real world.

Once she's got him in a compromising position, there are a number of variations to the game, depending on what it is the bad guys are trying to accomplish. If it's a spy thing, they may let it go long term so they can continue to extract information from their victim. The banker thing could also go a couple of ways. The woman could ask for his help, threatening to withhold her favors if he refuses. If that doesn't work, she can always go to plan B. Plan B would be to threaten to expose the relationship to the victim's family, specifically his wife.

It's important to note that the average blackmailer, although likely lacking a formal education, understands behavior and motivation better than Pavlov. For example, criminal blackmailers know that if the victim were to throw himself at the feet of his wife and confess, he'd probably be able to "walk it off."* Practicality would take over, and although he'd probably be paying the price for a long time, she'd forgive him. So the blackmailers always make sure of two things. First, they wait until the relationship has been going on for a few months before they make their play. That way, the victim can't use the "moment of weakness" excuse. Second, and this is very important, they will make sure that the victim has used the "L" word. That's right, L-O-V-E. Bad guys know that women know that men are inherently weak creatures. To a woman, sex is one thing, but if she ever finds out that you have been telling another woman that you love her, you're toast. The blackmailer won't have to explain this to the victim twice.

The blackmail technique is used against women, too, and is equally effective except for the fact that the love/sex thing is reversed. Guys might forgive their wives for loving another man but not for "giving lessons."**

But what if the intended victim doesn't go to bars or health clubs? Or what if he's smart (or experienced) and aware that this kind of thing happens? In the spy world, this is a big problem. People in sensitive government jobs receive training about this kind of approach and are expected to report any contact that might be a recruitment attempt by a foreign government. But spies have come up with unique ways of setting up "chance" encounters. A very popular one is to find out that the target is taking a flight overseas and arrange to place an operative in the seat next to him. Whether the goal is setting a honey trap or simply trying to make that first

---

* Although "walking it off" is normally used as a reference to a minor sports injury, on the street it means that you won't be permanently affected by an incident.

** "Giving lessons" refers to a married woman who is engaged in a sexual relationship with someone who is not her husband.

contact with a view to recruiting the target as a double,* a long airplane flight is generally conducive to getting acquainted.

Another innovative technique is called the "bump." The target's
car is located and the operative, in most cases a woman, simply
drives her car into his. She then goes to see him and apologizes,
promising to pay for everything. Within a day or two, the target is
compensated for the damages to his car. After a few days, the target
is placed under surveillance. Arrangements are made for the operative to have a "chance" meeting with the target, usually in a
restaurant or some other social situation. This can happen two or
three times. The ultimate result? A personal relationship blossoms,
in an apparently natural way.

If you're in business—and it doesn't have to be the financial
industry, you might be the guy who knows the secret formula for
Mountain Dew—just remember that lots of people from the spy
business are now in the crime business. They might be using these
methods on you!

For men, I have one suggestion that might help reduce the
chance of this happening to you. Tomorrow morning, before you get
into the shower, take off all of your clothes and stand in front of the
mirror. Then I want you to ask yourself this question: "Do I look like
Brad Pitt?" Chances are the answer is no, so when you're out and
about some night and an extremely attractive woman starts treating
you as if you do look like Brad Pitt—*wake up*!

Sex always works. Even the people who you don't think would fall
for it do. I knew this guy from Pakistan who took over as the new
general manager of a hotel. The hotel had about four hundred
rooms, as well as a pretty big health club on the top floor, with a spa
and a big swimming pool. There was also a bar on the top floor that

---

* A "double," or "double agent," is an intelligence officer spy who is recruited by the
enemy but remains in the employ of his own government.

was fairly popular with the Thursday after-work crowd. When the new GM took over, the health club wasn't making any money; nobody was joining and it was losing a ton of money.

The bar was set up in such a way that you had a pretty good view of the swimming pool. So the GM started a big promotion to get some of the local businessmen to join the health club. He hired half a dozen "models"* and made sure that they hung around the pool at the cocktail hour in their bikinis. Within a few weeks, after enrolment at the health club had gone way up, the GM canceled the models. After that, all there was left hanging around the pool was businessmen in their Speedos. Temptation isn't hard to resist; it's impossible to resist.

Many years ago, I worked this case where a guy went into a bank and applied for a $100,000 loan. When the manager asked him what he was going to use for collateral, he replied, "The weekend you spent at my brother's summer place." He got the loan. The manager had been set up. It cost the bank a hundred grand, since the crook never intended to service the loan anyway.

> You can get a lot farther with a kind word and a gun than a kind word alone.
>
> AL CAPONE
> *(1899–1947)*

In Mexico, they have a saying that they use when they are offering you a bribe: *"Plomo o plata?"* — "Lead or silver?" What it means is that if you don't take bribes, they will shoot you. Well, at least you get the option.

Just for a minute, stop reading and think about one of those secrets. Some awful, unspeakable thing that you've done that you really wouldn't like your friends, husband, wife or co-workers to know about. Now, chances are, you probably did this thing that you did, with somebody else. Unless you're really perverted, that is. And,

---

* Strippers

as the saying goes, the only way that two people can keep a secret is if one of them is dead. So what if some really unpleasant people were to find out about your dirty little secret or that of one of your employees? What would you do to keep it from getting out? What would your employee do?

My advice is to keep your eye on your employees. Not like Big Brother. More like a concerned friend. And if you think that they have a problem, try to help them out. People's personal problems do not go unnoticed by those who prey upon the weaknesses of others.

Six for Five

Mona works at a suburban bank branch and she's the ideal employee—smart, hardworking, cheerful and honest. Yet after she has been at the bank for ten years, she does something very strange. It's so out of character that none of her co-workers would believe it even if they knew about it, which they don't.

Mona has begun to allow certain people to make substantial cash deposits without requiring them to complete the necessary forms. She also makes sure that no suspicious transaction reports are filed. This goes on for several weeks. By the time she's finished, several million dollars of drug money have been deposited in an innocuous commercial account belonging to a "painting and decorating company."

What is going on?

What's going on is that Mona's husband has a gambling habit.

In some jurisdictions, the government controls gambling. Some places even have legal betting on sporting events. I once heard a government guy say that their sports betting system would eliminate illegal bookmaking in that jurisdiction. That made me laugh, because the only way that the government could push out the hard guys is to do what they do—give credit.

If you make bets with a bookmaker, he will extend you credit. In effect, you run a tab. If you're betting every day, and there are thousands of people who do, you will usually have seven days to make good on any debts you incur. You'll often hear bettors asking their bookie, "What's my bottom?" Your "bottom" is what you owe; it's derived from "bottom line."

But seven days is a short time and the world is full of people with weaknesses. If you get in over your head, you're "on the clock," which means interest is being charged, and you have to start, as they say on Wall Street, "servicing the debt." But this isn't Wall Street. On this street, the rate on unpaid accounts is "six for five." What this means is that if a gambler, let's call him Harry, bets $500 on the NFL game on Sunday and loses it, he has to settle before the following Sunday or he owes $600. It's basically 20 percent interest per week. About what I'm currently paying on my credit cards!

Now, to the bookie, let's call him Irving, servicing the debt means paying the "juice"* (interest) at least. If Harry does that, he can keep making bets. And to Harry, a degenerate gambler, that's all that really matters, because he *knows* that he's going to win big and be able to "straighten out" (pay) Irving. But as it turns out, Harry never does get that big win. He gets deeper and deeper into debt until eventually he can't even pay the interest.

Now Irving has a problem. If he lets Harry get away without paying, other bettors will think that Irving is a "pooch" (a person who commands no respect) and that they can do the same. Then there's anarchy!

So Irving sells Harry's account. And the kinds of people who buy these kinds of debts are usually very unpleasant. So those people go and visit Harry and they say, "Harry, give us a good reason why we

---

* "Juice" is the interest that must be paid on a loan. It is also referred to by the Yiddish word, "vigorish" or "vig."

shouldn't break your elbow." Harry has a hard time coming up with a good reason. They ask him how he is going to settle the now rapidly growing debt. He doesn't know. They ask him what he does for a living. He tells them that he is a truck driver. That doesn't do anything for them. Then they ask him what his wife does for a living. He tells them that she works in a bank.

All of a sudden, they're interested.

Later that night, Harry returns home. Mona doesn't know that he has already mortgaged their house. He tells her his tale of woe. He says that the bad guys have told him that if she doesn't cooperate, they will hurt him…maybe kill him.

What will Mona do? She's going to help her husband, of course. Sure, he's a bum. But she loves him. So, over the next several weeks, she accepts some very large cash deposits at the bank. The necessary forms aren't completed and no suspicious transaction reports are filed.

So how does a bank prevent this kind of scenario from playing out? One answer is to make sure that they have a good employee assistance program. Not something that everybody just pays lip service to—something real. If you have one, then maybe Mona can get help for Harry before things go too far.

The Strange Case of Robert Flahiff

If you decide to embark on a life of crime, there's one very important thing that you should know, and that thing is *everyone* is a potential informant against you—your wife, your mother, your brother, your lawyer, anyone you've ever worked for or worked with and anyone who has ever worked for you.

Judge not, that ye be not judged.
MATTHEW 7:1

The concept of "honor amongst thieves," "omerta" or the "code of silence," if it ever really existed, disappeared in the '60s when drugs came into fashion. Drug use and drug trafficking changed the profile of the average bad guy from hard-core criminal into sniveling loser; someone who, at the first indication that he's going to pull some time,* is ready to rat out anyone and everyone if it might shave some time off his sentence. Informants are the mainstay of criminal investigation, but they are treacherous and dangerous and can rarely be completely trusted.

Paul Larue was a mid-level trafficker in the 1990s. He ran cocaine out of Florida, and, as is usually the case if you deal dope long enough, he sold to the wrong guy. In this case, the wrong guy turned out to be a police officer and Larue took a "pinch"** for it. Pretty soon, he was telling the cops about who he could offer up in exchange for a break. This is pretty normal behavior when you're looking at twenty years in the "joint"† and cops don't always pay that much attention to it. But in this case they did; Larue told them he could give them a judge!

The judge, it turns out, was in Canada—Quebec, to be specific. Quebec is very much like Mexico without the nice weather. For some reason, there is much more corruption there than anywhere else in the country. Don't ask me why. I have some theories, but I won't air them here. When I was in the RCMP, the large majority of

---

* To "pull some time" is to receive a sentence, or a "bit." Once you've pulled your time, then you have to start "doing" your time. An archaic version of this is a "doing a stretch," getting "sent up" or going "up the river." "Going up the river" is an old New York term that refers to serving time at "Sing Sing," the state prison at Ossining, New York, which is up the Hudson River from NYC. The word "prison" itself may be avoided. Certain Italian organized crime groups will never use the word. When someone pulls some time, his friends will often say that he is "in Europe."

** To get "pinched" or to "take a pinch" means to be arrested.

† Unless you've been living in a cave all of your life and have never seen an old gangster movie, you'll know that the "joint" is prison. Also known as the can, the bucket or the Crowbar Hotel.

the corruption cases that we had were in Quebec or involved cops who were originally from Quebec.

While he was a lawyer, Judge Flahiff had apparently been a supporter of the correct political party, because in 1993 he was appointed to the bench of the Quebec Superior Court, which is a pretty big deal. When he was a lawyer, Larue was his client and Flahiff did a lot of Larue's banking for him. Between 1989 and 1991, Flahiff laundered $1.7 million in cash for Larue. The staff at the Bank of Montreal knew Flahiff so well that they'd let him into the branch after regular business hours with sports bags and briefcases full of cash. Flahiff bought bank drafts for Larue that were eventually deposited in a Swiss bank account.

Flahiff's defense was that he and his law partner were not aware of the nature of Larue's business. The prosecution took exception to the defense's argument and tendered evidence that Flahiff and his partner's nickname for Larue had been "Le Poudrier," a French term that means "the powder man."

Larue, in spite of "rolling over"[*] on "His Honor," got fourteen years for his trouble. Judge Flahiff, too, pulled some time of his own; he got three years. The funny thing was that Flahiff immediately appealed his conviction and refused to resign from the bench. He continued to collect his substantial salary even though he was suspended. The Judicial Council had to commence an inquiry into how to deal with this issue, since there were no specific regulations in place to deal with a money laundering judge. It just hadn't come up before—not even in Quebec!

Flahiff's lawyers argued quite eloquently, but he was eventually removed from the bench. In the end, he got flushed.

---

[*] "Rolling over" is another term for turning informant. Also referred to as "giving someone up." Both of these terms refer to accomplices. If you weren't involved in the crime, but know about it and inform, it is often referred to as "dimeing out" or "dropping a dime" on someone, the dime being the cost of the telephone call.

TERRORISTS

Whether a group is committing terrorist acts, trafficking drugs or laundering money, the one constant to remember is that they are all forms of organized crime.

STEVEN W. CASTEEL

Assistant Administrator for Intelligence,
Drug Enforcement Administration

It is important to recognize that we are dealing with two distinct and separate phenomena, linked mainly for convenience.

RAPHAEL PERL

Specialist in international affairs,
Congressional Research Service,
Library of Congress

Crime and Terror

The quotations above are from two smart men, one a cop, the other an academic. Their positions illustrate a long-standing argument on the nature of crime and terror. To an academic, crime and terrorism are separate concepts; statistics and words on a page. To a law enforcement officer, crime and terrorism are the two sides of the same coin, both victimizing innocent people.

Simply put, if you're on an airliner that is crashing into the sea, it doesn't really make a huge difference to you whether the guy who planted the bomb in the cargo hold was making a political statement or trying to kill a rival doper up in first class. Either way, you're still dead.

Every organized crime group on the planet got its start pursuing an ideology. Now, you may wonder, "What about outlaw motorcycle gangs?" Technically, the Hells Angels also got their start the same way. After World War II, the Angels were formed by veterans who decided that they wanted to "opt out" of regular "straight" society and committed themselves to what soon turned into a criminal lifestyle.

As for the Sicilian "Mafia," although historians argue about the specifics, the organization most certainly got its start as a political entity. One theory is that the word "Mafia" is an acronym for the words "Morte alla Francia Italia anela," which translates as "Death to the French is the Italian cry." But, whether they were fighting the French or working as muscle for rich landowners, they eventually morphed into what they are today—crooks!

These groups began with political or religious goals, or a mixture of both, but they either achieved these early ambitions or finally decided that they weren't very good goals in the first place. So then what do you do? It turns out that the transport, communication and logistical structures of a successful political, revolutionary or terrorist group are tailor-made for a criminal organization. So that's what most of them turn into.

Terrorist Financing

For years, law enforcement had been saying that the best way to go after terrorist groups was through money laundering investigations. The concept was simple. Take away their money and they're powerless. It took a tragedy, but after 9/11, everybody else finally caught on.

> It never troubles the wolf, how many the sheep may be.
> VIRGIL
> *(70–19 BC)*

Most people's ideas about terrorists, like their perceptions of organized crime, are drawn from TV and films. But contrary to the picture presented in the movies, the typical terrorist isn't a mastermind jet-setting around the world, or planning the downfall of Western civilization from the comfort of the oxygen bar at the Four Seasons. Criminals and terrorists aren't ultra-sophisticated manipulators of technology or financial geniuses. Shortly after 9/11, when airline stocks and a few others tumbled, somebody began to spread the rumor that the terrorists were shorting* those stocks. The press went crazy for it, but anyone in the game knew it was baloney. Terrorist groups don't think that way; they operate very much in a hand-to-mouth fashion. When they have money, they tend to spend it pretty quickly. The money arrives, they buy guns, bombs or airplane tickets, and the money is gone. They're not sticking it in a savings account! But they do, very often, make use of money launderers to get their funds across borders.

Up to a point, typical criminal money laundering and the financing of terrorist activity are exactly alike. The goal in both cases is to disguise the true source of the funds. Individuals contribute to terrorist groups in secrecy, and states that sponsor terrorism naturally prefer to remain in the shadows, since one of the repercussions of their exposure might be a "heat wave" in their capital city—at around 4,000 degrees—that wasn't in the weather forecast.

But there are significant differences between the two types of money laundering. The most obvious is the amount of cash involved: money is often tight for terrorist groups, and they don't have unlimited resources. Concealment of the proceeds of drug trafficking, on the other hand, can involve hundreds of complex financial transactions, because the dollars amounts are so high.

The fact that terrorist groups don't have much money sometimes works in investigators' favor. For example, the terrorists who planned and carried out the first attack on the World Trade Center, in 1992, were apprehended after trying to collect their deposit on the

---

* "Shorting," also known as "short selling," means you are betting that the price of a particular stock will go down. You can borrow stock from a broker and sell it immediately. When the stock price drops, you buy back the stock, give it back to the broker and pocket the difference. Don't try this at home unless you've got nerves of steel. If the price goes up, you can lose your shirt.

rental truck they had used to transport the explosive device. But the other side of that coin is that, as the 9/11 attacks or the Bali disco bombing demonstrated, the cost of mounting these kinds of operations is frighteningly low.

The truth is, the individual members of these terrorist groups are pretty much on their own when it comes to financing their activities. There have been a few big cases in which legitimate charities were hijacked or illegitimate ones created to raise funds, but more often the charity scam is used by groups that have more of a public image as a real political organization. An example would be the Liberation Tamil Tigers Elam, also known as the LTTE or LTT. This group is devoted to the liberation of their Tamil homeland in Sri Lanka. They are a sophisticated organization with most of the resources of a regular army.

Extortion disguised as political fundraising is an ever-popular method for terrorist groups. The Tamil Tigers used it for years— probably still use it. Bin Laden and the al Qaeda were doing it, too. If you're a politically moderate Arab businessman, what are you going to say when the terrorists come to see you and "ask" you to support them with a donation? Refuse this request and someone might let it slip that you are a "Zionist sympathizer."

Osama, Your Mama

Incidentally, when I say al Qaeda "were" using this technique, I am specifically referring to Osama bin Laden, because I think he's dead. I may be proven wrong, but I don't think so.

Think of it this way: if you were bin Laden and you wanted to give the finger to the United States, what would you do? You'd have your picture taken holding up a recent copy of the *Wall Street Journal* or *Hustler* or whatever it is those guys read in their caves to pass the time. So why hasn't bin Laden done that? Because he's dead, that's why. And consider the United States' position: if they had captured bin Laden alive, he would have been a huge security problem. Sticking him in Guantanamo wouldn't have helped, either; there are thousands of nut jobs out there who would be agitating or plotting, ready to do anything to get him released. And if they killed him and let the world know, it would be almost as bad. Then he becomes a martyr, and the same crazies would be blowing stuff up forever. *But if you kill him and then you don't tell anyone, you have deniability.* If every time Al-Jazeera releases some crappy tape, you can say, "Gee, that sure sounds like Osama," then he's like Elvis. You can't be a martyr if people think you're still alive!

In 1999 an Algerian "refugee" named Ahmed Ressam was arrested by U.S. Customs at the Washington State border. They found explosives in his possession that he planned to detonate at Los Angeles International Airport. By his own account, he was not financed by al Qaeda. In fact, he supported all of his own activities through petty crimes.

Here's what he said during his interrogation:

Q. What type of travel document did you use to get into Canada?

A. A fake French passport.

Q. What city did you go to?

A. To the city of Montreal.

Q. What happened when you arrived in Montreal?

A. Immigration stopped me.

Q. At the airport?

A. Yes. Immigration stopped me at the airport. At that time, I requested asylum.

Q. And how did you request—how did you request asylum?

A. I provided them with a false story about—to request

political asylum. They kept me at their center there and then they let me go.

Q. When they let you go, what city did you live in?

A. I lived in the city of Montreal.

Q. How long did you live in Montreal?

A. From 1994 to 1998.

. . .

Q. How did you support yourself during that four-year period?

A. I lived on welfare and theft.

Q. What do you mean by "theft"?

A. I used to steal tourists, rob tourists. I used to go to hotels and find their suitcases and steal them when they're not paying attention.

Q. And what would you do with the contents of those suit-cases?

A. I used to take the money, keep the money, and if there are passports, I would sell them, and if there are credit cards, I would use them up, and if there were any traveler's checks, I would use them or sell them.

The amazing thing about the Ressam case is that Canadian Immigration policy on refugees prevented the immigration officers from detaining Ressam at the "center" for longer than a few days. After that, he was released into the city of Montreal, unsupervised. They simply gave him directions to the welfare office and let him go.

Interestingly enough, the official police line on the Ressam case is that they had him under surveillance in Vancouver and then "lost" him. They contend that he turned up at the Washington border and that only the vigilance of a couple of U.S. Customs inspectors prevented him from actually getting to L.A. and putting a bomb down at the airport. I wasn't a cop when this happened, so I have no direct personal knowledge of the case, but I have to say that this version of the events sounds contrived. I am not saying that the authorities misled the media and the public just for the sake of doing so; there may have been deeper and perhaps nobler reasons for this deception, such as protecting a source. But I suspect the truth is that Ressam never really eluded the RCMP surveillance team at all.

I reiterate, this opinion is based solely upon conjecture. However, I have worked with surveillance teams everywhere and the RCMP has some of the best people in the world. There's no way that they would have lost Ressam. There is equipment that they would have used, which I won't describe here, that would have negated any chance they could lose him.

My theory is that the cops let him go so U.S. Customs could arrest him. Why? Probably because they knew that if they arrested him, they might not be allowed to hold him. The Canadian courts could have released him on bail—and then they would have lost him for sure. So they shooed him into the arms of U.S. Customs.

I would have done exactly the same thing. The Canadian legal system is so screwed up, so oriented towards the offender and his "rights," that Canadian law enforcement agents are frustrated beyond belief. It is a country where, almost by legislation, no one is obliged to take responsibility for their actions, where prisoners control the prison system and where the media have publicly ridiculed law enforcement for so long that the public has bought into it. Imagine political correctness taken to the absurd. A prison system in which a blind eye is turned to inmates injecting narcotics when they are not allowed to smoke cigarettes.

Ideology or Greed?

So what is the difference between a terrorist, a drug trafficker, a narco-terrorist, a revolutionary and a member of an organized crime group? I suggest that there is no difference; that all of the above are one and the same.

If you need proof, look at the situation in Colombia:

- March 2002—The U.S. government indicts Tomas Molina-Caracas for conspiring to manufacture and distribute cocaine with the intent and knowledge that it would be illegally imported into the United States. Molina-Caracas is no ordinary drug trafficker; he is the commander of the 16th Front of the Fuerzas Armadas Revolucionarias de Colombia (FARC), a leftist rebel group actively involved in terrorist attacks against the government of Colombia.
- June 2002—Police in Surinam arrest Carlos Bolas, reputed to be the leader of FARC. But Bolas isn't arrested for terrorist activity either; he is arrested for drug trafficking, as part of the same indictment against Molina-Caracas and their associates in Colombia and Brazil.
- September 2002—The U.S. government indicts three members of the Autodefensas Unidas de Colombia (AUC) for complicity in the movement of more than seventeen tons of cocaine into the United States and Europe between 1997 and 2002. The indictment states that the AUC members "directed cocaine production and distribution activities in AUC-controlled regions of Colombia." The AUC are a right-wing paramilitary terrorist group and the sworn enemies of FARC.
- November 2002—Pursuant to indictments that stemmed from an Organized Crime Drug Enforcement Task Force

(OCDETF) investigation out of Houston, Texas, two senior operatives of the AUC are arrested in Costa Rica, trying to exchange cocaine for arms.

- November 2002—Molina-Caracas's superior officer, Jorge Briceno-Suarez, commander of the eastern bloc of FARC, is indicted by the U.S. government for drug trafficking.[22]
- The leader of the AUC, Carlos Castano, stated publicly in 2000 that 70 percent of the AUC's activities were financed by drug trafficking. In fact, the DEA has identified members of both the AUC and FARC as being complicit in cocaine transshipment through Mexico and Venezuela.[23]

Both AUC and FARC lost sight of their political goals long ago—if they ever had any to begin with. It's about money and power, not freedom from government oppression or citizens' paramilitary self-defense. Both groups are using their drug proceeds to buy weapons so that they can defeat the government and take over the country. Then it'll be their turn to start mistreating the population—just like every other Latin American government has for the past two hundred years.

But it's not just the Colombians. The following "terrorist" organizations have also been shown to be involved in drug trafficking activities:

Abu Sayef
al Qaeda
ETA/Freedom for the Basque Homeland (Spain)
Hamas
Hezbollah
Irish Republican Army
Kosovo Liberation Army
Kurdistan Workers Party

Sendero Luminoso (Peru)
Tamil Tigers (Sri Lanka)
The United Wa State Army (Myanmar)

The methods of terrorist/crime groups tend to be the same and sometimes they swap "consultants" just like legitimate businesses. In April 2001, Niall Connolly, James Monaghan and Martin McCauley were arrested at Bogotá International Airport as they got off a flight from San Vicente del Caguan, a town in the Colombian demilitarized zone that is controlled by FARC. They were pretty far from the beach. So what were three Irishmen doing in Colombia, in FARC-held territory? Take a guess.

All three were traveling with false passports. When they were arrested, the Colombian police conducted a forensic examination of their clothing and found traces of explosives.[24] Connolly was the Latin American representative of Sinn Fein, based in Havana. Monaghan was a known IRA member who was convicted in 1971 for possessing explosives and conspiring to cause explosions. In 1982, McCauley was shot by the police when they raided an IRA weapons cache.[25]

Colombian President Andres Pastrana said that these men had been in Colombia training FARC members on mortar and bomb-making techniques. Not that FARC really needed any help in that department.

The moment that these guys were taken, everyone started pointing fingers at Sinn Fein, the political wing of the IRA, and its leader, Gerry Adams. In a letter to Congressman Henry Hyde, the chairman of the House International Relations Committee, Adams was unequivocal: "Let me state again to you that neither I nor anyone else in the Sinn Fein leadership were aware that the three men were traveling to Colombia."

Did the leaders of Sinn Fein know that the Three Stooges were teaching FARC how to blow things up more efficiently? Probably not. The peace process was already well underway in Northern Ireland. IRA brigades were voluntarily disarming themselves. So where does that leave you if you're an IRA bomb maker? Out in the cold, or in this case the warm, since it was Colombia.

Does this event mean that terrorist groups around the world are starting to link up? Of course they are. But, in this particular case, what it more likely means is that Connolly, the guy in Havana, was feeling lonely. According to a story in the *National Review*, the Sinn Fein office in Havana was being financed by the Cubans. It may have been at one time, but if you've been to Havana lately, you've seen that the Cubans are flat broke. The Russians don't give them money anymore—mainly because they don't have any. With no money and nothing to do, he may have seen the Colombian junket as an opportunity to stay in the game.

So he and the other two were probably just looking for an opportunity to make some money. Sinn Fein may well be the government in Northern Ireland some day, and there would be no room for these guys in an organization with new-found respectability. With peace in Northern Ireland, the guys who are committing the crimes, either the violent crimes or the money-making ones, will just keep doing the only thing that they know how to do, just like they do everywhere else. So it's very confusing. How many of the so-called terrorists actually care about a particular cause? How many of them are just trying to make money, gain power or both?

In the early 1980s, the members of the Medellin Cartel became so strong that they attempted to usurp the power of the existing democratically elected government simply by buying it. To avoid extradition to the U.S., they offered to pay off Colombia's national debt themselves (probably in cash...), get out of the drug trade forever and reinvest their offshore holdings back into the country. By doing this, they would effectively have controlled the economy of

Colombia. Just to be able to make an offer like that demonstrates that the cartel may well have been on its way to controlling the economy anyway. If the existing Colombian government, supported by the U.S., hadn't strongly supported extradition, the members of the cartel might have succeeded.

If your criminal activity is so successful that you develop the capacity to destabilize a government and take over a country, are you then a revolutionary or are you still just a criminal?

To best understand this, try and imagine a continuum, with pure ideology at one end and pure greed at the other.

I put it to you that every terrorist, and every professional criminal, for that matter, can be found somewhere on this continuum. Individual members of a group might be at very different places along the line at any given time, some being more concerned with religion or politics, others with making money. Yet there is one constant: no matter where you find someone along the continuum, there is always a concern with power. And, finally, no matter how strong a terrorist group's ideological convictions may be in the beginning, with the passage of time they will inevitably move along the continuum, away from ideology, toward greed. In other words, they will go from being terrorists to being organized criminals.

But whatever the state of the group's soul in its transit from "pure" to impure, there is always laundry to be done; the money that you amass by stealing or extortion to perpetuate your organization has to be washed clean.

So in the fight against terrorism and crime, knowing what motivates a particular group may not be that important, unless it allows you to predict their activities. What is important is what they are doing and how they are doing it.

Drug Dealing for the Cause

Methamphetamine, or speed, is a drug that has become increasingly popular, along with Ecstasy, in the dance club and rave scenes in major North American cities. In the '70s and '80s, most methamphetamine was produced in clandestine laboratories through an unstable and dangerous process involving the conversion of phenyl-2-propanone (P2P). In recent years, ephedrine, a compound found in cough syrup, has become the main precursor for methamphetamine production.

Speed is a big money maker. For a small investment, you can reap huge rewards. In January 2002, police arrested a number of men of "Middle Eastern descent" who had been smuggling ephedrine into the U.S. from Canada for conversion into speed, which they were trafficking in Chicago and Detroit. Law enforcement officials alleged that some of the proceeds from these activities were being sent to the Palestinian terrorist group, Hezbollah.

Another area of interest to drug investigators is the so-called Tri-Border Area—Paraguay, Argentina and Brazil—where a large number of Germans settled after World War II. By coincidence, there is also a very large and active Middle Eastern community, concentrated mostly around Ciudad del Este, Paraguay. Middle Eastern organized crime groups control most of the major criminal activity in the area, dealing in drugs and weapons and smuggling liquor and cigarettes. U.S. intelligence sources suspect that the Tri-Border Area is also the home of some important members of the Islamic fundamentalist terror groups Hamas and Hezbollah; their evidence for this is the flow of funds back to the Middle East.

Some questions are still unanswered. Are these criminals in Canada, the United States and South America actually members of Hamas and Hezbollah, or are they simply doing business with them? Are they themselves funneling money back to the Middle East to help subsidize terror, or are they simply facilitating the process by purchasing heroin, cigarettes and liquor from Middle Eastern associates who, in turn, use their profits to finance terrorism?

How's Your Mom?

Many people who are employed on the front line of the financial industry in North America are recent immigrants. These jobs do not pay all that well and they don't require all that much education. For that reason, they are ideal for people who have come to a new country and are trying to better themselves.

Most of these immigrants have loved ones back home. "Back home" is often not what we are all used to. Many of the countries they come from are lawless, unpleasant places, rife with crime, corruption and violence. And no doubt, among the tired and huddled masses of mostly honest people who emigrated, there were a few bandits and con men as well. There always are. When these bad guys get here, the first people they start committing crimes against are their former countrymen. After all, it's tough to extort from the rest of us if you don't speak English.

Newcomers to Western countries are often reluctant to report crimes because they distrust the authorities, particularly the police, who in many of those foreign countries are an organized crime gang unto themselves. So when a bank teller from Sri Lanka is approached by a member of a Tamil organized crime group and asked for money to help "the cause" back in the old country, does the teller call her supervisor at the bank and report it? Probably not, since, when the Tamil guy was politely asking for a contribution, he also mentioned that if there was anything that he or his friends could do for the bank teller's mom back home in Colombo, on So and So Street, she should just say the word.

Honey, I'm Home

Here's another popular way for terrorists to get their money around the world. People who are in the business of importing and exporting goods around the globe are nearly always obliged to deal with customs or some other kind of revenue-collecting agency, whenever the goods they trade in cross a border. To protect the general economic interests of the country and the domestic manufacturers of goods similar to those being imported, these agencies impose duties, taxes and tariffs. These charges are based on the type of goods and then, specifically, on the dollar value of the goods.

A common method of evading these charges is "undervaluation." This is exactly what it sounds like: telling customs officials that the things you are importing are worth less than they really are, and therefore paying less in duties and taxes. It's the most common customs fraud there is and costs governments literally hundreds of millions of dollars every year. Revenue agencies in developed countries have devoted great amounts of resources to detecting it.

But if you're a money launderer, it's also a great way to transfer money from one country to another. Let's say you're the money guy for a heroin trafficking organization in the southwestern United States and you need to get $2 million to Mexico. You have corporations on each side of the border that conduct legitimate business. You also have accounts and corporations in offshore financial centers.

To move the $2 million, your U.S. company purchases $2 million worth of concentrated detergent from a manufacturer in California. To make soap powder, concentrated detergent is normally bulked up with extenders such as soda ash and other fillers. A pound of concentrate might be enough to make twenty-five pounds of commercial soap powder.

Without diluting it, you repackage the concentrated detergent into containers, label it as commercial soap powder and ship it to

Mexico. On the bill of lading, the cargo is declared and valued as commercial soap powder with a value of approximately $40,000. If the Mexican customs officers examine the load, they will see that it is, in fact, soap. It would be difficult for them to determine the level of concentration.

The agents in Mexico receive the shipment, add the appropriate dilutants, repackage it and sell it on the market as commercial soap powder. From their initial $40,000 purchase, the Mexicans will realize close to $2 million of profit from the sale of an innocuous commodity. You will have successfully transferred the money and quite likely won't have aroused any suspicion. This kind of thing goes on every day, in every country in the world, and it's very difficult to detect

It also works the other way. If you need to get money from someone, all you have to do is "overvalue" an item. Get them to buy something from you that is of little value but is difficult to appraise, a carpet, for example. For $250,000, you sell them a carpet that is really worth only $5,000. They send you the $250K as payment for the "expensive" carpet. They have to pay customs duties on it, but that's simply the cost of doing business. These groups would pay substantially more than that to clean up their cash by other means anyway.

Let's take another scenario. Suppose that you work for the spy service of an unnamed Middle Eastern country. Your government wants to support a particular political organization (translation: terrorist group) in another Middle Eastern country but still wants to be perceived as a "friendly nation" by the United States. So, using one of the front corporations that your spy service has in place, you sell a tanker full of olive oil to a front corporation that the political group has set up. You sell them cold-pressed, extra virgin olive oil, worth $100 a liter, but you undervalue it: you describe it on the export documents as twelfth-pressing crap that you wouldn't use on the gears of your ten-speed. They sell the oil at a substantial profit and use the money to buy explosives, which ultimately end up in vests worn by seventeen-year-old children the group has brainwashed into becoming suicide bombers.

One month after 9/11, two Florida International University professors, John Zdanowicz and Simon Pak, released the results of an interesting study. Their analysis of U.S. trade data for 2000 indicated that the prices for honey exported to Yemen, the United Arab Emirates, Kuwait and Saudi Arabia were substantially higher per kilo than for other countries. What this means is that terrorists based in the U.S. could have been using the overvaluation technique to raise money for their activities. In one case, Zdanowicz and Pak looked at twelve shipments of honey from Charleston, South Carolina, to Yemen. For those shipments, the price that the Yemenis paid was 38 percent higher than the average price of honey exported from the U.S.[25] Another interesting fact is that Yemen produces some of the highest-quality honey in the world, so why would they want to import honey from South Carolina in the first place? Maybe the answer lies in Yemen's long history as a popular haunt for terrorists, fundamentalists and spoiled rich kids from Europe, trying their best to embarrass their parents.

The thing to remember is that this is terrorism, not drug trafficking. It doesn't take a whole bunch of money to put together the average terrorist operation—$100,000 might be enough to do it. If you're a bank that is in the middle of these transactions, you would never be able to tell, simply from observing the money flow, that this is a money laundering scheme. The only way to avoid becoming involved in something like this is to make sure that you don't take bad guys on as clients in the first place. And that's more easily said than done. To prevent money laundering in international trade would take considerable effort on the part of law enforcement agencies and customs offices. You would have to track every import and export transaction in the same way that banks are required to track and report financial transactions. The up side is that customs would then detect significant amounts of fraud as well.

But if you want to catch money launderers, this is where they are: in business, dealing in boring things like soap powder or honey or bicycles or magnets.

A Cache for Cash

Terrorism and organized crime are abstract concepts to most people, since they rarely notice when they rub up against them. But it is important to note that ordinary citizens and small businesses can also play an important role in the prevention and detection of money laundering. This story involves a relatively minor amount of money, and the transaction wouldn't have surpassed the reporting threshold, if there was one for car dealers, but it certainly qualifies as "suspicious."[26]

On Thursday, July 13, 1996, a truck dealer in Peterborough, England, received a phone call from a man with a pronounced Irish accent, saying that he wanted to buy a truck he had seen on the dealer's premises. They agreed on a price of £2,000. The customer said he would pay for the vehicle in cash and send the payment to the dealer later that day. He also said he would call the dealer back and make arrangements to pick up the truck. Towards the end of the day, a courier arrived with the payment as promised, in cash.

The following day, Friday, July 14, the man with the Irish accent called the dealer again. He told the dealer that he would be delayed and might not be able to get up to Peterborough until later in the evening. He asked if there was any chance that the dealer could simply have someone leave the truck at a nearby car park, unlocked, with the keys under the seat. The customer agreed to take responsibility for the truck in the event that there was any damage or it was stolen. Since the truck had been fully paid for at this point, the dealer did what the customer asked. Some time during the late evening, the truck was collected from the car park.

The following day, Saturday, July 15, the truck was parked on a street in the business district of Manchester, England. Concealed inside the vehicle were several hundred kilos of high-caliber explosives. The bomb was detonated, causing many injuries and millions of dollars worth of property damage.

The man who set up the deal for the truck had an Irish accent, paid in cash and structured the deal so that he remained completely anonymous. This transaction took place at a time in England when IRA bombs were going off almost every week. Yet the truck dealer never thought to report the transaction to the police. Why? Was he going to pocket the money and avoid paying the tax? Maybe. But more likely it never occurred to an honest guy, just trying to get through his busy day, that the deal was strange. If the British government in 1996 was not able to stir up public awareness about terror and money laundering, in a country that was virtually at war with the IRA, how are other governments supposed to do it today?

DOMESTIC BANKING AND SECURITIES

Do financial institutions have a role to play in the prevention of money laundering? Absolutely.

But financial institutions are not the police. They are in the business of making money, and their role, despite what the regulators may say, is not one of enforcement.

Now, having granted them that, I maintain that there are still many things that a financial institution can do to detect crime. And if they assist law enforcement, they'll be helping themselves at the same time.

Not doing business with criminals is, in fact, good business.

KYC = CYA

One of the most significant issues in money laundering prevention is the "Know your customer" rule. Bankers call it KYC. I call it CYA, which stands for "Cover your ass," because that's what most of them are really doing.

> There is a history in all men's lives.
> *Henry IV, Part 2*
> WILLIAM SHAKESPEARE
> *(1565–1616)*

What it means is that if you're going to do business with someone, you need to know who you are dealing with and what they do for a living. This isn't a complicated concept, but in spite of their best efforts, most financial institutions don't have it right. The other day, I went to the bank to open a business account. The lady who opened it had obviously been given some kind of money laundering compliance training recently, as she was being very officious about looking at my driver's license and then at me to see if the picture matched. But a real money launderer would have slid right past her and she would never have known. She missed the whole point of the exercise. What should have been of interest to her was the fact that I was an existing customer opening a new account. I already had an account. Why did I want a new one? Why was I changing the nature of my dealings with the bank? That kind of thing is exactly what should start a bank thinking KYC. Why is the customer doing this?

When an existing customer changes things or when a new customer comes in to establish a relationship, it's the perfect opportunity to obtain information: to develop a profile of just exactly what he is planning to do with his account, the sources of the money and what services he will require of the bank. It's perfectly acceptable for a bank to ask a customer about his business and the types of transactions he will be doing. And that doesn't only mean asking if he or she plans to make large cash deposits or foreign wire transfers.

Once you have established a profile of the customer, it becomes easier to spot suspicious transactions if he or she starts to display a pattern of activity that is a departure from the norm. It's also a good way to detect fraud, either by the customer or one being perpetrated on the customer. In smaller branches, where the staff know their customers, they can often tell that their elderly clients are being victimized by con artists when they come in looking for a large draft or a certified check.

Money launderers need to get their money into the banking system. To do this, they need bank accounts. Most financial institutions are big and impersonal, and bad guys are looking to take advantage of that. If they can set up the account without having to provide too much information, they can operate fairly anonymously. Once they have the account, the bank may never see them in person again.

Some banks still maintain what are known as "lodge accounts." These are accounts that are established for charities, sports teams and not-for-profit organizations that regularly receive donations from large numbers of people. They are perfect for low-level laundering because, typically, the account traffic involves deposits of cash or third-party checks, which subsequently move out of the account in the form of an instrument of some type. This kind of activity is sometimes referred to as "warehousing" and it is a strong indicator of money laundering activity.

If a launderer needs to open multiple accounts, another technique is to pay a "beard"* to open the account and then just take it over. Either that, or simply establish an account in another name using false identification.

So how does a bank get its employees to do the things that are necessary to prevent and detect money laundering? Obviously, the answer is training. But the hard part is training people not just to go through the motions, but to *think*.

One day a few years back, when I was still in the money laundering business, I went into a bank in Canada at which I maintained, on behalf of U.S. Customs and the FBI, a number of corporate bank accounts that my colleagues and I used to warehouse criminals' funds while they thought we were investing and cleaning it up for them. I was making a deposit of a comparatively small amount of cash, about $50,000, we had earned as commission on one of our deals. When I approached the teller, a young man about twenty-five or so, with my deposit slip and the cash, he slid a source-of-funds (SOF) declaration form across the counter to me.

In those days, there was no legislation in Canada that obliged financial institutions to report suspicious transactions or transactions

---

* A "beard" is an intermediary who is used to conceal the actual participant in a transaction or communication.

over a threshold amount. Not only that, but government hadn't yet established a reporting center to record and analyze reports, so there wasn't any place to send them anyway. But the banks took it upon themselves to start having some of their customers fill out forms just the same; the forms were then sent on to their own security people for review. According to the rumor, banks were aware that the government was about to pass legislation forcing them to report wires and cash transactions over $10,000, and they hoped their voluntary action would delay the new laws. The bankers were smart. They guessed that money laundering legislation was going to cost them a fortune, because it would oblige them to create a huge infrastructure just to remain in compliance. They were right. Now that there is legislation, they spend a ton of money on obeying the law and it doesn't make them a cent in profits.

Anyway, the young teller gives me the form. Now, you have to remember I'm supposed to be this big gangster, so I can't just say nothing and fill out the form. I had to act like a gangster. So I thought that maybe I'd try blustering my way out of it, and maybe intimidate him a bit while I was at it, just to keep my skills up.

> *Me:* What the fuck is this?
>
> *Teller:* This is a source-of-funds declaration, sir. It has to be completed for every cash transaction over $10,000.
>
> *Me:* I'm not filling this out.
>
> *Teller:* I'm sorry, sir, it's bank policy. You have to complete the form or I can't take your money.
>
> *Me:* Listen, man, look me up on your computer there. I have about ten different accounts at this bank with about a million bucks in each one, so don't try to fuck me around. You'll just end up stubbing your dick and getting fired.
>
> *Teller:* Sir, If I take your money without having you fill in the form, I'll get fired anyway.

This kid was pretty good, and he wasn't having any of my bullshit.

So I filled out the form. In the space where it said to put your name, I printed "Brian Mulroney," who was the prime minister of Canada at the time. Then I gave the form back to the teller. He took the form, thanked me and placed it in the appropriate slot. He never even looked at it. Obviously, no one else ever did, either, because the bank never called me on it and none of them knew who I really was.

That was the problem. The teller's training had worked right up until the point where he got me to fill out the SOF form. But it doesn't do much good to force customers to do the paperwork if you're not going to take the time to look at it when it's completed. It's still all about training people to think. A novel concept, I admit, but a good one.

A King or a Kingpin?

There is one special class of customer that can pose a danger to a financial institution. Bankers call them "potentates." The FATF calls them "politically exposed persons." These are heads of government or state: kings, presidents, high-ranking government officials and the like. They usually have substantial holdings. When you're a private banker, landing a client like this means huge profits.

However, the origin of the money may be questionable. If you're a politician in a corrupt country, and you steal, you don't have to bother laundering the money. Your position makes you—as the Romans described their emperor—*ultra vires*: above the law. You may still move the money around from bank to bank, but not to launder it. It's usually so you can "piece off"* all of your cronies. If

---

* To "piece off" a person is to provide them with a fee for services rendered, or their "piece" of the action.

you can't be prosecuted, you can do whatever you want. At least, that's your perception when you are the absolute ruler of a country. But political power is often fleeting.

For the bank, everything will go famously until the potentate falls from power, or turns out to be a supporter of terrorists or a mass murderer or a drug trafficker. Then the private banker gets his or her name in the papers, and business goes bad. Sometimes it may not be possible for a bank to refuse a potentate's business; there may be political pressures from the government, for instance. However, proper due diligence, and risk assessment of these and all other potential new accounts, can significantly reduce the risk.

The way to do this is through the technique mentioned above: "profiling." Since 9/11, profiling has become a bad word: civil liberties groups and some Arab associations have denounced it as a racist tactic that singles out individuals—specifically, visible minorities—on the basis of their ethnicity. And there have been a number of incidents where these groups have probably been right. Although I have been sent for a secondary search at the airport on a few occasions, I often couldn't help thinking that they were searching me simply so the number of Caucasians matched the number of non-whites who were being checked.

Like anything else, profiling can be abused by those with their own agendas or prejudices, but, if practiced properly, it can be an effective technique to identify high-risk individuals, whether they're boarding a plane or opening a bank account.

Take Miami International Airport, for example. U.S. Customs at Miami have an outstanding record of narcotics smuggling arrests. Some people say it's because almost everyone that gets off the plane in Miami is carrying drugs! But, be that as it may, the Miami airport team uses profiling to identify thousands of individuals every year who are attempting to smuggle contraband into the United States. But instead of targeting individuals of a particular ethnic group, true profiling focuses on things like a person's country of origin or the country they've visited. Specifically, they are looking for people who are returning from narcotics source or transshipment locales.

The problem is that a country like Nigeria, for example, is both a source country and a transshipment point for narcotics. Nigerians are notorious among law enforcement agencies around the world, including the Nigerian Federal Police, for being associated with narcotics smuggling, particularly heroin. They are also of interest due to their historic involvement in advance fee, or "419," frauds. ("419" frauds, named after a particular section of the Nigerian criminal statutes, are those letters and emails that everyone gets, purporting to be from the deposed leader of an African country who wants to share $20 million with you.)

Purposely failing to distinguish between prejudice and informed vigilance is the tactic that opponents of profiling use so they can play the race card. Certainly, law enforcement agents will be on the alert when it comes to Nigerians. But that is simply an intelligent assessment of the facts, not a vindictive desire to prejudge individual cases. In a case like this, the problem is

Common sense is in spite of, not as the result of, education
VICTOR HUGO
(1802–85)

that there are very few white Nigerians, so when the police become suspicious and send a Nigerian to secondary inspection, they are also sending a black person. This kind of logic is very easily abused, of course, and it is hugely important that law enforcement officers keep this in the front of their minds. Believe me when I say that it is drilled into them over and over. Nobody wants to be accused of being a racist. Guilty or not, it's a tough label to get rid of.

If you are operating a financial institution, profiling is equally a matter of common sense. Every person who comes through the door should be closely scrutinized before a new account is opened. This is of particular importance in the offshore jurisdictions, but it also applies to every branch of every domestic bank, no matter the size. Now, granted, if you're operating a small branch in the middle of Oklahoma, the chances of Osama bin Laden's brother-in-law coming in and opening a checking account are slim, but these techniques will still help you reduce the incidence of other things like fraud.

Here are a few questions that should be asked:

What is the country of origin? Transparency International is an international non-governmental organization devoted to combating corruption. Their website[*] features their International Corruption Perception Index, a list of the countries of the world in order of how corrupt they are perceived to be. Obviously, it would be impossible to measure corruption with any kind of scientific accuracy. This list is the result of a survey of the observations and experiences of people who conduct business internationally. According to their 2002 survey, starting with the most corrupt, these countries are the worst:

1. Bangladesh
2. Nigeria
3. Paraguay
4. Madagascar
5. Angola
6. Kenya
7. Indonesia
8. Azerbaijan
9. Uganda
10. Moldova
11. Haiti
12. Ecuador

[*] www.transparency.org

13. Cameroon
14. Bolivia
15. Kazakhstan
16. Vietnam
17. Ukraine
18. Georgia
19. Venezuela
20. Nicaragua
21. Guatemala
22. Albania
23. Zambia
24. Romania
25. Philippines

What this means is that if you're a financial institution, you really should be very careful when you transact business with people or companies from these countries. And if you're interested in laundering money, it stands to reason that your chances of being able to do that in such high-corruption places are pretty good. Coincidentally, a number of these countries have also appeared on, or are still on, the FATF list of non-cooperative countries and territories. The list changes all the time, but if you check the FATF website at www.fatf-gafi.org, you can see who is currently in the penalty box.

Who referred the customer? Quite often, financial institutions will accept a referral from a law firm or some other well-known institution as sufficient proof of a customer's bona fides. In fact, the money laundering laws in some jurisdictions, the Cayman Islands, for example, will allow a bank to rely on the due diligence of another foreign bank if that country is listed on the appendix of countries that are considered to have sufficient legislation—which of course may be a mistake.

Either way, if you rely on someone else's work, make sure that you at least call them to confirm it. If you've never heard of the bank or referring entity, make sure that it exists. Letterhead can be stolen or created on a computer, so it's also a good idea to speak directly with the person who has signed the letter of reference. Make sure that you get a letter or an email from them confirming everything that you spoke of.

If the letter of reference has the phone number of the referring entity on it, take the time to look up the number yourself. There's a very common fraud, often based on the correct assumption that bank employees are lazy and will use the number in front of them instead of looking it up. The way it works is that the bad guy will apply for a loan and provide proof of the existence of some other monetary instrument he will use as collateral. Often it will be a form, purportedly from a bank or insurance company, that says the applicant has, for example, a certificate of deposit (CD) for $100,000. The bank employee is then supposed to confirm the existence of the collateral before advancing the monies.

The bad guy will have created the form himself: it will indicate the address and phone number of the branch where the collateral is supposedly held. But the phone number will be for a phone that the bad guy has set up himself. He's pretty sure that the bank employee, who is required to call the branch to confirm the existence of the CD, will not bother to look up the branch's phone number independently. He or she will just dial the number that is on the form. Someone will answer, saying "Such-and-such Bank, how can I help you?" The person will then go away to "check," and return to confirm the existence of the fictitious CD. The bad guy gets his loan, the bank loses its money, and you and I end up paying a bit more each month to use the ATM.

Is there a legitimate and logical reason to establish this account? You need to ask why the person or company is establishing a banking relationship with you. Where did the customer bank previously? Did he close his accounts because the tellers were ugly or did they punt him because of suspicious activity? You need to know this before you proceed.

Is the entity incorporated in a foreign country? If it is, what is the nature and scope of the business that they will be doing in your country? Who are their local customers, partners and suppliers? If the company is incorporated in a foreign country that appears on the FATF list or the Transparency International corruption list, or is a country with corporate secrecy, be careful. Ask a lot of questions. Bad guys really hate questions.

What kind of activity will there be in this account? Wire transfers of lire to Lesotho? Monthly movements of Krugerrands to Kuwait? It's very important to determine at the outset what the customer will be doing with the account. This is your chance to grill him on his activities, because once the account is established, it will be hard to get him back in front of you. For example, will there be any cash deposits? If so, how often and in what amounts? Once you've established the customer's profile, then the account can be monitored by your bank's suspicious transaction detection software, or the old-fashioned way, by a human being. Either way, if there is any change in the activity in the account, you can catch it.

Another thing that bankers should watch out for is the use of safety deposit boxes by criminals. What better place to store your swag? It's also a great place to stash your cash if you're making a drug buy. Excellent security, no prying eyes, and the people you're purchasing from won't try to rip you off inside a bank. Bankers should always keep an eye on who's visiting their box a little too frequently. There's a good chance they're up to something.

What is the customer's line of business? Obviously, you have to be on the lookout when potential customers operate cash-intensive businesses, such as restaurants, hotels, parking lots and the like, but it's important that you not lose sight of other factors. Banks operating offshore should be very careful when approached by government officials, members of law enforcement and intelligence agencies or the military. These guys shouldn't be opening offshore accounts and, when they approach a private bank (that is, a bank that offers personalized financial services for rich people), where the minimum deposit is quite often in the millions of dollars, the question that begs to be asked is, "Where did they get their money?" Chances are, they got it from doing something illegal.

Some years ago, I was entertaining two visiting Thai police officers in Toronto; one was a general and the other, as I recall, was a colonel. After lunch, as I was driving them to another meeting, we passed a very exclusive private girls' school. The colonel said something like, "Oh, that's where it is." I asked him what his interest was and he replied that his daughter attended that school. The cost of sending a child from Thailand to an exclusive girls' boarding school in Canada was probably, at the time, five or ten times more than this police colonel was officially earning. There's always the chance that he was legitimately wealthy, but in those countries, rich people don't join the cops. Quite often, though, people join the cops to become rich.

The Four (+1) Basic Principles of Money Laundering Compliance

For those of you employed in a financial institution, this is important. These are the essentials of money laundering compliance. I call them "four (+1)" because I added an extra one. They are:

1. A designated money laundering compliance officer;
2. A complete set of anti-money-laundering compliance rules, regulations and procedures;
3. Regular and comprehensive training for all employees;
4. Independent testing of the anti-money-laundering safeguards; and
5. (The extra one) appropriate suspicious transaction detection software.

The designated money laundering compliance officer. The person who does this job can be called a "compliance officer" or a "money laundering reporting officer" (MLRO), but more often the term "pain in the ass" springs to his co-workers' minds. In spite of being absolutely necessary, he is generally considered a nuisance by the financial services industry. Talk about a thankless job. Typically, the people MLROs supervise see them as an impediment to business. And the board of directors and the executive level of an institution see them as the appropriate people to take the heat if there is ever any kind of money laundering problem, because they must not have been vigilant enough.

In some countries, being responsible for anti-money-laundering compliance can even be dangerous. When I was in Colombia, a senior banking official once asked me how many bodyguards a compliance officer in my country would employ. Apparently, down there, they are getting knocked off all the time.

What qualifications are required to be an MLRO? In some places, the assumption seems to be that anybody can do it. In most organizations, being the MLRO is not the person's only responsibility and, depending on how the role is perceived by that institution, it could be assigned to anyone from the in-house legal counsel right down to the guy who fills the soap dispensers in the men's room.

Anti-money-laundering compliance rules, regulations and procedures. Companies in the financial services sector are very good at creating rules and protocols for every possible eventuality. They are closely regulated and usually have people who are really good at coming up with lists of things you are not allowed to do. As well, in most countries, the money laundering reporting authorities will provide a template and the organization just has to fill in the blanks.

Regular and comprehensive training for all employees. Since financial institutions are still considered to be the front line in the fight against money laundering, they're under a lot of pressure to ensure that their employees are appropriately trained to detect it and they know it's a really big problem. So how do banks train their thousands and thousands of employees to recognize potential money laundering violations? The answer is, they don't. What they do is give them some training sessions that are so boring the employees can hardly stay awake for them. The "training" is usually focused solely on the idea that money laundering is about criminals making cash deposits. After which, they scare the hell out of them by saying that if they do something wrong, they could go to jail. Then they tell them to have a nice day and send them back to work.

There are several reasons for these deficiencies in training. First, money laundering compliance costs money and takes time. The banks know that, when the regulators come for an inspection, the first thing they will ask the staff is, "Have you had training and when?" The regulators won't be concerned with the quality of the training; they'll just tick the box and say that the institution is following the rules.

Second, many of the people who provide the training haven't got a clue what money laundering is. Often they're just reading from a book or a training manual. When I was in the Cayman Islands giving some training to the staff of a medium-sized bank, they couldn't close the bank for the number of hours the course took, so we split the people into two groups and I simply gave the same course twice. We trained more than three-quarters of the staff that week. The bank's training person (also their human resources person) sat through both sessions. At the end of it, she asked me for a copy of my notes and presentation. She said that she was going to give the training to the remaining staff herself. I figured that she didn't know any more than the rest of the people who had attended, except that she had sat through it twice. I told her that I wasn't teaching CPR, that you need experience to answer people's questions on the subject. She was a nice lady, but her training sessions would have caused more confusion than Father's Day in the housing projects.

And that's the issue. Training has to be comprehensive and interactive; above all, it must train the employees to think. Training people to think? What a concept!

Independent testing of the anti-money-laundering safeguards. This is another one that's open to different types of interpretation. Just exactly what does "independent" mean in this context? For a large institution, it could very well mean verification by their internal audit people. For smaller ones, it means using the "C" word—consultants. For a not-so-small fee, you can hire a consultant, usually from the forensic division of one of the major accounting firms, to conduct a review of all of your money laundering prevention activity. Now, if they send over a bunch of accountants to do the review, chances are they'll identify some deficiencies in things like your policies and reporting procedures. But these days, most of the big accounting firms hire former police officers, sometimes former money laundering investigators, to help with the review. You can be sure that those guys will find even more. When they're actually working,[*] the former cops will uncover stuff you never dreamed of. It's worth the extra cost, and it's infinitely better to hear from them how many problems you have than to hear it from the regulators when it's too late.

Know Your Employees

Knowing your customers (KYC) is important, but it's equally important to KYE—know your employees. Most organizations conduct a background check when they hire a new person, but typically, when something bad happens, the problem isn't the employee himself but one of his friends, relatives or associates.

> Those you trust the most, can steal the most.
> LAWRENCE LIEF,
> *Industrial security analyst*

The problem is, how far do you go? Is it feasible, or even realistic, to conduct a background check on every person that your new employee associates with or is related to? The short answer is no. So how do you reduce the chances of hiring people whose brothers, sisters, lovers or friends are criminals? Well, you could start with an enhanced personal history when a new employee is engaged. You have them fill out a lengthy form that identifies immediate family members, friends and associates. Even better is to use a professional interviewer, who can substantially reduce your risk of hiring someone with criminal associates by asking the appropriate questions during the initial employment interview.

The only fully effective way to keep criminals and money launderers out of a bank is to lock the doors and let no one in. And since you can't do that, it's important to come up with methods to reduce exposure. Simply put, the threat of money laundering will be greatly

[*] And not hitting on your female staff

reduced if you don't let the bad guys into the bank in the first place.

When I do speaking engagements, I often ask the audience, "How many of you have ever met a member of organized crime?" Sometimes one or two people will say that they have, but the reality, and also my reason for asking them the question in the first place, is to explain to them that they likely wouldn't know a gangster if they saw one. Almost everyone's images of crime and criminality are shaped by popular culture—by films and television. The reality can look very different.

The Muffin Man

Criminals don't have to infiltrate a bank by getting one of their own people hired. There are other ways to get around an institution's defenses.

> One may smile, and smile, and be a villain.
> *Hamlet*
> WILLIAM SHAKESPEARE
> *(1564–1616)*

When I was laundering, the police had provided the executives at the banks with a "letter of comfort." This document was their assurance that they could process the transactions we directed to them and not have to worry about being prosecuted for being complicit in money laundering. So, at the most senior level, the banks were aware of our activities. However, at the lower levels, specifically the branches, they were completely unaware of who we were. And in those days, even though there was no specific legislation requiring the banks to have customers fill out source-of-funds declarations, many banks had voluntarily decided that they were going to do so anyway.

Nevertheless, I went into the banks on countless occasions and made huge cash deposits, and only once was I ever asked to fill in a form. How did I do it?

When somebody has a problem at a bank, who do they deal with?

If there's a problem, who gets yelled at? The tellers, of course, and maybe a few other front-line people. Nobody really treats those people with any respect. They meet hundreds of people every day, many of whom are in a hurry, in a bad mood or both. It's just not that pleasant.

I figured out that if you were nice to them, there was probably a pretty good chance they would do things for you that they wouldn't normally do for a customer. I took it upon myself to be friendly and attentive to every bank employee I met. Especially those on the wire transfer desk. I kept notes on my interactions with them: how many kids they had, what their vacation plans were, if little Johnny played soccer, etc. Then, before I went into the bank next time, I'd check out which employee was on duty, refresh my memory by a peek at my notes, and go in smiling and friendly. I'd ask the teller if her husband's arm had healed after he fell off the roof two months ago, and she would think that I'd actually remembered and say to herself, "What a nice man that Chris is..."

I would bring the employees muffins. Believe me, nobody does that for them. I would share personal information with them about my wife, children, etc.

Once I told the lady at the wire desk about how one of the kids was sick and had to get tubes in his ears. Later that day, I telephoned her and said, "I am at the hospital with my youngest, getting another prescription for an ear infection. Do you think that you could transfer $300,000 from one of my accounts and wire it to that same Panamanian construction company as last week? I'll come in later and sign the documents."

"Sure, Chris, for you, no problem!"

Total investment, four dollars for muffins. Where did I learn this technique? From the bad guys, of course.

Here's another example of the "muffin man" technique, this one from a genuine bad guy. In the mid-1990s, the DEA and the RCMP were investigating a Guyanese drug trafficking group that was importing multi-kilo cocaine loads into the United States and Canada, using a seafood business in Toronto as a front to conceal their activities. The company transacted a significant amount of business at a local bank branch, and Everton, the company's owner, was soon a familiar face, well known to all of the staff.

Everton was a likeable, even charismatic guy; he became very friendly with the female branch manager, Roxanne, who coincidentally was also Guyanese. Everton eventually introduced Roxanne to his wife, and she, in turn, introduced Everton and his wife to her husband. With the passage of time, the two couples became friends; they often socialized together, visiting one another's homes, going to dinners, attending baby showers, etc. One day, Everton and his wife contacted Roxanne, saying they had something very important to discuss with her and her husband. When they met, Everton and his wife asked the bank manager and her husband if they would do them the honor of becoming godparents to their new baby. Asking you to become the godparent to someone's child is probably the biggest compliment that anyone can pay you. What it means is that those making the request admire your character and values so much they would want you to raise their child in the event that they could not. Who could refuse such a request? Certainly not Roxanne and her husband. They agreed and became the godparents.

Within six weeks of the christening, Roxanne was taking large cash deposits from the seafood company at her home! Everton, who was actually a drug trafficker, had co-opted this woman to the point that she couldn't refuse his request. After all, they were friends and she wasn't really doing anything wrong. He just didn't have time to make the deposit, what with a new baby and all. This is not, by the way, the first time that I have seen criminals make use of their children as pawns in some larger plan. I know this notorious arsonist and con man who was always on the fringe of Italian organized crime was trying to be accepted. He converted from Judaism to

Catholicism just so he could get a certain organized crime figure to be godfather to his child. (Harold, if you're reading this, I'm talking about you!)

Was Roxanne, the Guyanese bank manager, foolish to trust her new friend so much? Yes, she was. But was she a criminal? By definition, yes. But not at first. Criminal behavior is a continuum. Often, a person will embark on this continuum with actions that are motivated by loyalty or kindness—looking the other way when someone steals, failing to report a colleague's drug use on the job—and tells himself he has done nobody any real harm. Continued association with criminals, however, even if you don't know they are criminals, will typically move you farther along the continuum, little by little, until one day you wake up and find yourself doing things that you never dreamed you could do. It's a very gradual process.

I am convinced that it is this same process that caused ordinary German soldiers to participate in unspeakable atrocities in World War II.

The Securities Market

It isn't only banks that have trouble with compliance. The capital markets are where all our money is: yours and mine, pension funds, personal invest-

> The mob has never seen a market it didn't want to manipulate.
>
> SPECIAL AGENT JAMES KALLSTROM, FBI, New York

ments, everything. We put it there because it's supposed to be secure. If the integrity of the market comes into question because of scandals and losses, "investor confidence" disappears, which means, in real terms, that people will put their money in their mattress instead of into the economy. The result can be a recession, or worse, a depression. So governments in general, and agencies of the government in particular, such as the U.S. Securities and Exchange Commission, spend a huge amount of time and effort trying to keep the crooks out.

But the bad guys are always looking for ways in. Manipulating the price of securities is very attractive to criminals because there is so much potential profit. But unlike other things that the bad guys do, such as drug trafficking and theft, securities manipulation provides a method to legitimize, in fact launder, the illegal profits you make. You can't really go to the IRS and tell them that you made a million dollars selling cocaine, but you can tell them that you made it from buying stock at a low price and selling it when it went up. Nothing wrong with that. That's one of the reasons why organized crime has become so interested in it. The other reason is the huge amounts of money you can make if you can figure out ways to change the price of a stock.

And when the bad guys start looking for ways to get at the good guys' money, you can be sure there will be trouble. In the securities industry, where pretty well everyone's income is derived from the commissions earned on sales, it's sometimes tough to get people to buy into the whole compliance thing. And although it causes huge problems at the other end, some brokers will still take on new customers without checking them out; some will still even take cash from them. Typically, it's a lot easier to rationalize breaking the rules, or even the law, when there's a client sitting across from you who has the potential to help you make your next five mortgage payments.

Because selling stock is a very lucrative business and also a very competitive one, it's not only the lower-level employees who are tempted to cut corners. In business, if you're not growing, you're dying. So companies, looking to expand, sometimes have to find new sources of capital. Organized crime is always ready to provide loans to publicly traded companies that are in debt or need capital to expand their businesses. But once you're "in the soup" with these guys, chances are you'll never get out.

HealthTech International was a small, publicly traded company located in Mesa, Arizona. They owned and operated a chain of health clubs in Texas, Arizona and Oregon. Their stock was trading at 63 cents a share and going nowhere. To improve the price, a senior executive of the company, made a deal with three "stock consultants," Eugene Lombardo, Claudio Iodice and Irwin Schneider. They agreed to increase the stock price and get paid off in HealthTech shares.

Now, here's another good example of where a little due diligence would have helped. First of all, what the hell is a stock consultant anyway? In this case, it meant that these guys were crooks. Lombardo was an associate of Frank Lino (a.k.a. "Curly" Lino), a capo in the Bonanno organized crime family. Schneider was a disbarred securities lawyer. A whole crew of other mob guys were also in on the deal and the HealthTech people should have seen it coming. It doesn't take a whole lot of due diligence to figure out that if you get into business with guys with names like "Green Eyes," "Boobie" and "Meat Face," there are going to be problems.

Lombardo set up a scam with a broker at a firm in Long Island. According to the federal indictment, the broker in Long Island and some of his guys agreed to tout HealthTech stock to customers in return for commissions and bribes.

These guys were good. On the very first day that they started pushing the stock, there was a fourfold increase in trading volume; the share price went from 88 cents to $1.34, an increase of 53 percent.

The senior executive "straightened out" Lombardo, Iodice and Schneider by giving them hundreds of thousands of shares and warrants. Over the next few weeks, they dumped their holdings and made out like the bandits they were.

The rest of the story is pretty predictable. This operation was a classic pump and dump. The mob guys employed boiler-room tactics and drove the stock up to $3.06. At this point, the executive apparently started to get nervous. He went to the wiseguys and told them that he didn't want to continue.

They weren't sympathetic. Iodice simply told him that he would knife his wife if he didn't cooperate. So he kept cooperating.

The bad guys made tons of money; the unwitting victims lost everything. The HealthTech executives went to jail and people lost just a little bit more faith in the stock markets.

Cash-Intensive Businesses

Businesses that deposit cash receipts daily are obviously high-risk customers for a bank. The proceeds of criminal activity could easily be mixed in with legitimate income. But if the bank's profiling is thorough, the account's customer activity can be compared to the activities of other customers in similar lines of business.

For example, let's say that Supermarket A, an independent grocery store, has demonstrated a gradual shift in deposit activity so that it now makes 60 percent of its deposits in cash, 15 percent in food stamps, 10 percent in credit card slips and 15 percent in checks. You, the bank manager, decide to compare the deposit pattern to another client, Supermarket B, which is part of a grocery chain. Supermarket B makes only 10 percent of its deposits in cash, with the rest equally divided between checks and credit cards. In spite of the change in activity, Supermarket A has not demonstrated an increase in gross revenues. Supermarket B has shown impressive increases in revenues.

Because Supermarket A is an independent, the owner can do as he chooses and doesn't have to answer to anyone. Supermarket B, on the other hand, is simply one store in a nationwide chain of several hundred. The manager doesn't have a lot of latitude and operates his business as his head office directs.

The owner of Supermarket A is a native of Colombia and hires Latin American employees almost exclusively. The manager of Supermarket B is not a foreigner and has lived in the city his entire life. His family members all do business with your bank.

You learn that the brother of the owner of Supermarket A operates a *casa de cambio* (currency exchange) that sends money to Latin America. The brother does not do business at your bank.

After comparing the two, you become concerned. Your fear is that the owner of Supermarket A may be exchanging customers' checks for cash provided by the brother who operates the currency exchange. Cash that you are now convinced is being deposited by Colombian drug traffickers.

You file a suspicious transaction report on Supermarket A.

However, what you have been doing is comparing apples to oranges. Here is what you don't know: Supermarket A is located in an older section of the city with a diverse ethnic population. And that means more food stamps and more people who pay cash for their purchases. There aren't too many credit cards down in the projects!

Supermarket B, in contrast, is in a fairly well-to-do area of the city. No food stamps here. Most people pay with checks or their credit cards.

But the reality is that the owner of Supermarket A is an honest, hardworking citizen. He has two children; his daughter is a doctor and his son is an FBI agent. The manager of Supermarket B (that's right...the white guy!) has a part interest in an escort service and has been using the merchant number of Supermarket B to process transactions for the prostitutes, who, thanks to him, are now able to accept all major credit cards.

The increase in revenues at Supermarket B is a result of the commingling of legitimate revenues with the proceeds of an illegal act, disguised as legitimate credit card transactions.

Nothing is ever what it seems.

Smurfs

In most jurisdictions, customers completing cash transactions of $10,000 or more are obliged to fill in some kind of document identifying the source of the funds. This is called "threshold transaction reporting." Some people say that all a threshold like this does is give the money launderers a benchmark they know they must stay below to circumvent the reporting structure. Bearing this in mind, a bank employee should remember that a deposit over the threshold may be quite normal, while a smaller deposit is possibly the one that should raise suspicion. Any judgment about whether a transaction is or is not suspicious should be based on a number of different factors.

A technique that was employed at one time, mostly by Colombians or people working with them, was called "smurfing." The idea was this: you take a large sum of cash and break it down into smaller, digestible amounts. Less than $10,000, of course. Then you distribute these small amounts of cash among a veritable small army of smurfs (innocuous-looking plain folks), who convert the cash into negotiable instruments or sometimes just exchange small bills for larger ones. They arrive in an area of the city and scatter everywhere, buying traveler's checks, postal money orders, bearer checks, etc., and at the end of the day, they turn everything back to the launderers and get paid. The reason the operatives were called smurfs was that the bad guys would often use elderly people, mostly "blue-haired" old ladies, to do the work. Hence the name.

A Dominican group in New York City once negotiated with some friends of mine at the DEA to have them smurf their $1 bill action from crack sales. Just doing the $1 bills, they were laundering as much as $1 million per month.

Lots of people like to mention this technique when they make presentations or speeches on money laundering, but the reality is it was never that popular a technique. Those old people are tough to manage. Their memories aren't all that reliable, and apparently they would get lost a lot or lose track of time. It was like herding cats!

OFFSHORE BANKING

Taxes are what we pay for a civilized society.

OLIVER WENDELL HOLMES
(1809–94)

How much is a billion? The best way I've found to understand it is this:

- one million seconds = eleven and a half days
- one billion seconds = thirty-one years

In 2001, the Federal Reserve Bank of New York calculated that there was more than US$800 billion on deposit in Grand Cayman. That is equivalent to:

- twice the amount of money on deposit in all of the banks in New York City
- nearly 20 percent of all of the deposits in the United States
- $3,000 for each man, woman and child in the United States

The Fed also calculated that this amount is increasing at a rate of $120 billion each year.[27] And that's just Grand Cayman.

Years ago, there were dozens of low-tax and zero-tax jurisdictions that catered to those wishing to walk the line between tax avoidance and tax evasion (I like to call it "tax avoision").

But each year, fewer and fewer places are prepared to offer these services. The Cayman Islands have signed a tax disclosure agreement with the IRS and the U.K. Inland Revenue to exchange tax information on "persons of interest."[28] All of the countries identified by the FATF as "non-cooperative territories" are frantically amending their laws to avoid sanctions by the developed countries. So it's getting tougher and tougher to hide your money, even if you made it legitimately.

People who go offshore with their assets, for a number of reasons, both legal and not so legal, include:

- criminals hiding their illegal earnings
- corporations and individuals avoiding creditors
- persons wishing to trade in securities without disclosing their identities
- professionals such as dentists and doctors (particularly surgeons) who fear enormous malpractice judgments
- persons of great wealth who wish to minimize the taxability of their assets when their estate is passed to their children
- otherwise law-abiding citizens who wish to conceal assets from the income tax collectors

Why Go Offshore?

There was a lot of talk during the Enron implosion about Cayman and the idea of going offshore. The Enron people (so it is alleged) used offshore corporations to conceal transactions, in order to falsify their financial statements and keep the stock price up. An inflated stock price allows the senior executives of a corporation to continue to receive gigantic performance bonuses, because the company seems to be doing well. They refer to these transactions as "off–balance sheet" transactions.

What the hell is an "off–balance sheet transaction"? It is, simply, a deal that is done but not reported on the financial statements. Are they common? Apparently they were until the SEC started to crack down on so many public companies. Are they ethical? The answer to that question is this: Go home tonight and tell your wife that you are having an "off–balance sheet" relationship with your secretary and see what happens.

The money laundering part of the whole Enron thing apparently involved hiding debt offshore. Certain transactions were conducted in a tax haven, which legitimized the proceeds of what was essentially fraudulent activity. The executives then (allegedly)* reaped the rewards in the form of increased salaries and bonuses, as well as stock that they could then sell at the artificially inflated price and make even more money.

It has also been alleged in the Enron case that the senior executives were able to convince their accountants to certify the correctness of the financial statements when they were, in fact, not accurate. The government contended that Enron's executives had their accountants over a barrel, because the accounting firm, Arthur Andersen, not only did their books but also had profitable consulting contracts with the company. If the Andersen partners refused to allow certain questionable accounting practices, they ran the risk of being fired as auditors and losing all that valuable consulting work. And they couldn't be expected to give that up, could they?

Again, it was all about money.

Notwithstanding what has been said in the press, the accounting profession is still made up of honest, ethical people. Even the Arthur Andersen thing was only a couple of guys. But it killed their firm and put a lot of very good people out on the street—the very same street that the Enron employees got thrown onto through no fault of their own.

---

* Please remember that, at the time of this book's printing, not everyone has been convicted, so in regard to them, everything is still "alleged."

Currency Smuggling

If criminals find it difficult or impossible to inject their cash into the electronic banking system because they are operating in countries that have instituted strong anti-money-laundering structures, they have various ways of moving the cash out physically. Many of them resort to smuggling large amounts of currency out of the country they are based in and into a jurisdiction with less stringent banking regulations or a more corrupt infrastructure.

However, in most countries, you are obliged to advise customs of any amounts of cash, over a threshold, that you are taking out of the country. If you don't, and they find it, you'll get done for a currency violation. You won't be charged with money laundering. It won't be that complicated. The money will be seized, and you won't be getting it back.

Smuggling currency is very much like smuggling any other illegal commodity. You can use couriers or you can conceal it in another legal shipment.

Using couriers is a very risky business. Anyone stupid enough to act as a courier probably isn't that reliable in the first place. If they get caught, you certainly won't want them to know very much about the drug trafficking group that they work for because it's a good bet that they will cooperate with the police. You might think that a lot of couriers would simply abscond with the money, but that rarely happens, for one very good reason: couriers are usually within the same ethnic group and/or nationality as the rest of the criminal group, and they know that if they take off with the cash, somebody else in their family will end up "paying the price."

Most couriers, if they are caught, come up with pretty unconvincing stories. And the money isn't usually very well hidden either. Some friends of mine with U.S. Customs had been having great success picking off money shipments at the airport in San Francisco, and I thought that it might work in Canada. So one Friday afternoon, a couple of the guys went down to the airport to see what they could find. They noticed that there was a flight to Cartagena, Colombia, up on the board and they figured that might be a good place to start.

They went down into the bowels of the airport and started pulling luggage that was destined for Colombia off the belt. One of the first bags that they checked had $400,000 hidden in it!

They immediately went upstairs and interviewed the owner of the bag, who, of course, knew absolutely nothing about any money. At that time, there was no law to hold him on, so they had to let him go. What he said when he got to Colombia, I have no idea. But try explaining to a bunch of drug traffickers how *you* got on the plane, but the money didn't. And to make things worse, tell them the cops took it, and explain why you don't have a receipt.

Once the money is seized, a lawyer will usually show up with some incredibly stupid story about how this money has nothing to do with drugs, that his client won it at the casino or it was a gift from a friend or some other baloney. On one occasion, the cops grabbed this Jamaican guy in the departure lounge, heading for Kingston. In his bag was eighteen grand in twenties and tens. It was seized and he was sent on his way.

His lawyer called to say that his client was on his way to buy a backhoe in Jamaica, that this was the money to pay for it and, as they always say, "This is how business is done down there." Like the cops are morons. Like the lawyer has ever done business in Jamaica...

The thing that the cops didn't tell the lawyer was that there was a small cube of hashish, probably only a gram or two, that had somehow gotten squished in between the bills when they wrapped them. So in this case, it wasn't a big stretch, tying the money to drugs.

In the U.S., they use specially trained dogs that can sniff out currency. Some of them are good, but the statistics on detector dogs are not that reliable, whether it's for drugs or money or explosives. What often happens, when a seizure is made, is that the dog handler is there with his dog anyway. Even if the dog wasn't instrumental in finding the contraband, the handler will try to get the dog credit for the find. The investigators don't care. In fact, if they actually received the information from an informant, they often prefer to report that "the dog found it." It keeps their informant in the clear, and the dog people get to prove, once again, how necessary they are. Then their bosses can make a case for more personnel. I don't mean to imply that the dogs don't do a good job. They do. It's just that they too are part of a huge bureaucracy.

The Black Market Peso Exchange

According to U.S. Customs Service estimates, American citizens spend upwards of $57 billion every year on the purchase of narcotics.[29] With the current population, that's about $200 a person. The figures are pretty similar in Canada, and it's mostly in cash.*

Organizations that deal in large quantities of narcotics and cash have big foreign exchange challenges. They need to repatriate the majority of their profits back to the drug source country to pay for the merchandise, transport, security, etc. They also want to be able to spend it. In many countries—Colombia and India, for example— they have strict foreign exchange controls. The bad guys want to circumvent these controls whenever possible and, at the same time, they also want to maximize their profits.

Another issue for large international groups is that they generate

---

* I didn't buy any dope this year and chances are, if you're reading this book, neither did you. So there must be some guy out there who bought $600 worth in the past twelve months.

huge amounts of local currency in the various countries where they traffic drugs, so they also have to deal with converting that currency. Some people may request payment in U.S. dollars. Some may want Colombian pesos. Whatever they want, there is a high degree of exposure at this first part of the process of laundering money, the placement stage.

In response to this, Latin American money launderers adopted a method that had been used for many years to transfer wealth, circumvent exchange controls and make a healthy profit all at the same time. It's called the black market peso exchange (BMPE). Here's how it works. The drug traffickers in Colombia sell their drugs in the United States (or any other country) and generate cash, which a BMPE broker then agrees to buy from them. Agents in the U.S. deliver the dollars to the BMPE broker's U.S. representatives. Payment in pesos is then made to the trafficker, back in Colombia. The BMPE broker will charge a fee for this that can run anywhere from 5 to 25 percent but is usually around 10 percent.

The BMPE broker in Colombia is now holding a large position in U.S. dollars that are physically located in the United States. Using a variety of techniques, the BMPE broker will inject the cash into the banking system. Typically, he'll own a business in Colombia that purports to be an import/export firm. It doesn't take too much brainpower to figure out that it's just a front, but that doesn't seem to stop legitimate Colombian merchants from doing business with them. Of course, the Colombian definition of "legitimate" can differ greatly from the one that you and I are familiar with. Although they may not be directly involved in criminal activity, business operators who deal with the BMPEs know that they are complicit in the international movement of drugs and money. The Colombian merchants will place orders for all types of consumer goods and the BMPE broker will purchase them from U.S. vendors, either through personal contacts or by means of a U.S. front business.

Whatever way the goods are acquired, the BMPE broker will then ship the goods to Colombia via a number of other countries; Panama is particularly popular. From there, the Colombian importers will smuggle the goods into Colombia and distribute them. The BMPE broker receives Colombian pesos for this service in place of the pesos he gave to the drug traffickers in the first place.

> A holding company is a thing where you hand an accomplice the goods while the policeman searches you.
> WILL ROGERS
> (1879–1935)

It's very easy for a North American company to become unwittingly involved with these schemes. The biggest thing to watch out for is the settling of outstanding accounts by third parties or in cash. When you're in business, the most important thing to you is getting paid, so it may not be that big an issue for you if the company that pays your bill is not the same company that the merchandise was shipped to. But if this happens, there's a very strong chance that you may be involved in a BMPE money laundering scheme.

The Much Maligned Cayman Islands

Just as our perception of crime and criminals is shaped by popular culture, so is our perception of the countries where these crimes take place. To most people, if you're from Texas, you're a cowboy; if you're from Colombia, you're a drug trafficker; and if you're from the Cayman Islands, you're a money launderer. At one time, it might have been true.

The Cayman Islands opted to remain under British rule when Jamaica became independent in 1962. Though very small (93 square miles) the colony has countless banks, and for many years had a reputation as a tax haven for the wealthy and as a safe place for criminals to launder cash. But in recent years, things have changed, and today it's harder to launder money in Cayman than it is in the United States! Admittedly, they were a bit slow off the mark when it came to getting their money laundering laws together, but when the FATF took them to task for it, placing them on their first list of non-cooperative countries and territories, they reacted with surprising speed. The government quickly passed money laundering legislation and wasted no time getting itself removed from the list.

These days, if you walk off the street into a private bank in the Cayman Islands and ask to open an account, chances are they'll hand you a brochure and politely show you the door. These things have to be done in a civilized fashion: first, you need to make an appointment. Second, for most private banks, you'll need to have a few million in assets that you wish to have them look after. And third, despite what John Grisham says, it better not be in cash or they'll call the cops!

Cayman has worked very hard at making itself a respectable "off-shore financial center," which is, by the way, what all of the countries that used to be called "tax havens" now call themselves.

The whole thing turns on the issue of privacy. Please remember that when I say privacy, I am referring here to business and financial activity, not to who you've seen naked. There are those who argue that privacy is a basic human right and should be protected by law. Most civilized countries have, or are developing, legislation to make this so. But the difference between privacy and secrecy has to be recognized. Important as it is that all citizens have the right to privacy, it is equally important that no citizen should have the right to secrecy, if that secrecy means that the government cannot access your information, even with judicial authorization.

Confidentiality of an individual's personal financial affairs is legislated in Cayman and a breach of this law is a very serious offense. Years ago, Cayman banks were aware that many of their clients were failing to report their worldwide income to the tax officials of their home countries. They certainly weren't about to report them, but after a time, the banks began to advise their clients verbally that they were obliged to report their income to the taxman. That evolved into a situation in which new clients were obliged to sign a document acknowledging that they had been so advised. The current climate is such that new clients are advised, and must sign a statement acknowledging that they have been advised, that the Cayman court will order that their bank records be produced if a foreign authority is able to provide reasonable grounds.

The Cayman government realized that allowing court-authorized access to bank records was the only way to ensure that their bank confidentiality practices would be able to survive. This wasn't about tax evasion; it was about laundering the proceeds of serious criminal activity. It was about drug trafficking. Many people felt that drug traffickers and other international criminals were getting the message that they and their money were not welcome in the Cayman Islands.

> If you are out to describe the truth, leave elegance to the tailor.
> ALBERT EINSTEIN
> (1879–1955)

Dope dealers and professional money launderers have known for a long time that Cayman is definitely not the place to go anymore if you're looking to clean up your coke money. The trouble is, this reality hasn't yet filtered down to all the corporate types who want to hide their insider trading profits from the IRS—as the Enron case demonstrated.

The Name Is Gibbs...Brian Gibbs

Until quite recently, there were a few bad guys still actively laundering the fruits of their labors through the Cayman Islands banks.
They'd been doing it for a long time and apparently hadn't heard it
was time to go elsewhere. This fact had not gone unnoticed by certain agencies of the U.K. government, specifically MI6, the British
Secret Intelligence Service.

To get in step with other jurisdictions, reinforce their new legislation and continue to send the message to criminals that the
Cayman Islands government was serious about combating money
laundering, the Cayman Islands government established their own
financial reporting unit. The director of this unit was Brian Gibbs, a
former member of the London Metropolitan Police (a.k.a. Scotland
Yard—which since moving to its current address in 1967 has been
called "New" Scotland Yard). Gibbs was a very experienced cop, having spent twenty-five years on the streets investigating everything
from drugs to homicide. He had set up the first drugs profit confis-
cation unit (DPCU) at New Scotland Yard in the mid 1980s and as a
result found himself seconded to the Royal Cayman Islands Police
(RCIP) in the late 1980s to help them do the same. This unit is now
known internationally as CAYFIN (Cayman Islands Financial
Reporting Unit). Eventually, Gibbs retired from the Metropolitan
Police and became CAYFIN's civilian director.

One of the biggest money laundering cases that the RCIP investigated was the case against four officers of EuroBank, a private
Cayman-based financial institution.

The story begins in California in 1997, when Kenneth Taves, the
operator of an Internet porn site, approached a bank in California
and purchased the credit card information of 900,000 of its customers. At the time, it was a fairly common thing for banks to sell
this kind of information; for obvious reasons, they don't do it

anymore. What the people at the California bank didn't know was that Taves had a criminal record. He had a conviction for passing counterfeit checks and another for being an accessory to murder.

Once he got the credit card numbers, it was a pretty simple thing to bill them each $19.95 through his porn site. Before he got caught, he'd collected $35 million.

There have been other sites, usually porn or gambling sites, that have done this kind of thing. Not that I would know this from personal experience, but there are some so-called free adult content sites on the Internet where you will be asked for a credit card number as proof that you are over eighteen, as per the requirements of the Children's Online Protection Act. This is a scam. They don't care if you're over eighteen or not; they simply want to grab your credit card number. In 2001, the *Los Angeles Times* reported that Crescent Publishing, the publishers of *Playgirl* magazine, were ordered by the U.S. Federal Trade Commission (FTC) to refund $30 million in charges they improperly billed to visitors to their various sites. People who used their credit cards to sign on to *Playgirl*'s "free peep show" ended up getting billed for recurring monthly charges of $90. The *Playgirl* people made $188 million in two years off this scheme. The brilliance of it was that, if the victims noticed the charges, they would be too embarrassed to contest them. I think Playgirl.com was mostly naked men, so, whether you were a man or a woman, you might have been be reluctant to admit that you were on the Internet checking out guys in fur chaps!

Anyway, Taves got caught and the FTC sued him for fraud in 1999. The courts ordered him to disclose all of his assets, which he did, except for $23.5 million on deposit at EuroBank in the Cayman Islands, which he forgot to mention. He eventually pleaded guilty, and when a receiver was appointed, the Cayman account was discovered. EuroBank was served with an order restraining it from disposing of the funds.

The next development created a huge scandal in Cayman and Britain. The RCIP alleged that Taves had been making personal payments to an officer of EuroBank and charged four of their executives with money laundering.

In an unrelated case that soon became related, it turned out that the U.K. government was very interested in the activities of certain international criminals, particularly Russians, and had been pursuing an intelligence operation against them, code-named "Victory." Their main source of information was an employee of EuroBank in Cayman who, as in every good spy story, had a code name, too: "Warlock."

Warlock was secretly gathering information on account holders and passing that information on through his local handler, none other than Brian Gibbs! Officially working for the Cayman Islands police, Gibbs was also moonlighting for the U.K. government; he had been receiving information from Warlock about a number of individuals and it was eventually disclosed that he was forwarding a large amount of it to "an agency of the U.K. government," which everyone immediately guessed was MI6.

There were rumors he had placed wiretaps on all sorts of people. *Offshore Alert*, a U.S. newsletter that covers money laundering and fraud issues in the Caribbean, reported that Gibbs had been intercepting* the private electronic communications of certain individuals on the Cayman Islands under the authority of the various governors and attorneys general. Elected members of the Cayman government were reportedly kept in the dark about these activities. But the funny thing about Cayman is that, for a place that is known internationally for confidentiality, everyone sure seems to know everyone else's business!

One morning in early 2002, a prominent member of the Cayman

---

* Wiretapping

Islands judiciary arrived in his office and found a troubling message on his voicemail. It wasn't a message, really; it was a recording of a conversation he'd the previous night at a social event. The judge likely thought that an anonymous friend at Cable & Wireless, the local telephone service provider, was giving him a "heads up" that he was being spied on. (*Offshore Alert* also reported that Cable & Wireless assisted Gibbs in legally intercepting private communications and that they sought, and received, an indemnity from prosecution from the governor.) His Honor immediately contacted the RCIP and an investigation was commenced. If the Cayman judiciary was being bugged, Brian Gibbs was an obvious suspect.

Gibbs's witness statement in the trial of the EuroBank Four explained that, one evening in June, he received a telephone call from a representative of the U.K. government, advising him that the RCIP were about to execute a search warrant on his house and office. Gibbs's relationship with MI6 was important enough to the U.K. government that they told him to destroy all documents that linked him to them. This included debriefing reports of source Warlock, the main information source on the EuroBank money laundering prosecution.

Warlock and Gibbs's relationship was material to the defense's case. Gibbs was obliged to reveal all. In fact, an MI6 agent, who would only identify himself in court as "John Doe," actually came to Cayman and testified in the case. Doe eventually declared that Gibbs had destroyed the evidence of his relationship with Warlock on orders from MI6.

This disclosure was so prejudicial to the prosecution's case that all charges against the defendants were thrown out. Brian Gibbs left Cayman, followed not too long after by the attorney-general.

So how did MI6 know in advance that the RCIP were about to execute a search warrant on Gibbs's residence and office? Were the RCIP the subject of a wiretap, too?

And what about the "intercept" on the judge? After a lengthy investigation, it turned out, according to one of my sources, that while the judge and his wife had been at a social event, she had accidentally pressed the "redial" button on her mobile phone and inadvertently called her husband's voicemail at work, effectively recording their conversation. Given the prevailing atmosphere at the time, anyone might have come to the same conclusion. So, in the end, maybe he wasn't being bugged. But, if not, he may have been the only one who wasn't.

Russia

In the final years leading up to the fall of the Soviet Union, high-ranking government officials stole everything that wasn't nailed down. Once the government collapsed, all the state-run companies were privatized. What that really meant was that, overnight, people with the right connections became the owners of companies that they had previously just managed, many of them becoming instant millionaires in the process. Now, if you are one of these people, what do you do next? Get your money out of Russia, of course, and into your foreign bank accounts, usually in tax havens and countries with bank secrecy laws.

And that's where it went. The deputy chairman of the Central Bank of Russia stated that in 1998 alone, almost $70 billion was transferred from banks in Russia to banks in Nauru.[30]

Where the hell is Nauru?

If you care, and most people don't, Nauru is a tiny island in the Pacific, south of the Marshall Islands. It's also the world's smallest independent republic. It has a population of about 12,000 people[31] and a large proportion of them must be bankers. Until recently, the island's only industry was the export of phosphates (bird droppings) for fertilizer. When that started to run out, they switched to offshore banks and anonymous corporations. Nauru became a charter member of the FATF's list of non-cooperative countries and territories (NCCTs), remaining on the list for all four of their NCCT reviews. No small amount of political pressure was placed on the government of Nauru, with the result that they passed legislation in March 2003 to abolish offshore shell banks. They then advised the FATF that they had revoked the licenses of all remaining offshore banks. The FATF's response to the government of Nauru was that, although they "welcomed" these efforts, they asked them to "take additional steps" to ensure that those banks are "no longer conducting banking activity and are no longer in existence."[32] Basically, what they said was the international equivalent of "Prove it."

In December of 2003, Nauru finally was able to prove it and the FATF took them off the list.

But whether the money is in Nauru or some other discreet hiding place, it certainly isn't in Russia anymore. According to some estimates, from 1986 until 1999, there may have been as much as $500 billion looted from the country by corrupt politicians, intelligence officers and organized crime. They must have seen the end coming because they started stealing it more than two years before the Communists were deposed. Between 1989 and 1991, the Soviet Union's foreign currency reserves went from $15 billion to $1 billion and their gold reserves went from 1,300 tons down to 300 tons.[33] That's a thousand tons, or two million pounds, of gold! Now, a typical gold bar weighs

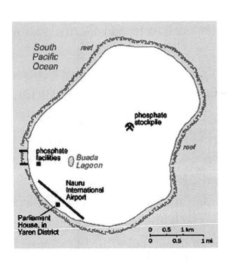

about 400 ounces; that's 25 pounds. So these guys had to steal 80,000 gold bars, each weighing 25 pounds. I sure hope that there was a hernia clinic in Nauru!

But that's not all. They didn't just steal the Russian people's money, they stole ours, too. In 1998, the International Monetary Fund (IMF), in an attempt to help stabilize the ruble, loaned the Russian government $4.8 billion.

Yuri Skuratov, the former Russian prosecutor-general, stated publicly that almost the entire amount was stolen. According to Skuratov, the money was sent to eighteen different banks, at least one of which, he alleged, was controlled by associates of the former Russian president, Boris Yeltsin.[34]

In response to this whistle-blowing, the FSB, the Russian Federal Security Service (formerly known as the KGB), released a video of Skuratov doing the "horizontal mambo" with two prostitutes. It was reported in the media that these women were, in fact, in the employ of the FSB.[35]

Like every other honest man in Russia, Skuratov was defeated. He was suspended by Yeltsin, and then ultimately fired by Vladimir Putin, Yeltsin's appointee and a former KGB big shot.

All that money that the IMF throws around belongs to you and me. All of the so-called First World countries pony up billions of dollars every year for projects like this. But the countries that need this kind of help are usually screwed up because their leaders are pissing away their countries' money. Little African nations where the leader is always shown on TV wearing one of those leather bellhop caps like Eddie Murphy and Jim Brown wear, shooing flies away with a horsehair wand. Countries where the people are starving, yet the president has a dozen palaces, a huge army and embassies everywhere. A visit to the UN plaza in New York City will confirm the old bodyguard adage that "the crappiest countries have the biggest limos."

The Russian press reported that $1.4 billion of the IMF money went through the Bank of New York and then on to its Geneva branch, Intermaritime. From there, it was allegedly deposited into an account at a Russian bank known as the "United Bank."[36] One of the purported owners of the accounts was Boris Berezovsky, an infamous Yeltsin associate who may be the richest man in Russia—another person whom Skuratov tried, and failed, to indict.[37]

Ukraine

At the time I am writing this, the Ukrainians just got off the FATF blacklist because they just passed money laundering legislation. I say, big deal. Ukraine is still one of the most corrupt countries in the world. Their politicians, as the saying goes, make their money the old-fashioned way—they steal it!

A former prime minister, Pavel Lazarenko, stole huge amounts of cash from the country and then bought Eddie Murphy's old house in California. The government of the Ukraine has spent a fortune in legal fees trying to recover the money that this guy stole and then laundered through a bunch of countries.

Recently, there was a case in Canada where a company hired a Russian guy to look after its accounting department. He was a pretty diligent worker. He stayed late most every night and rarely took vacation.* It turned out that, because this company didn't segregate the employees' duties, he was able to wire-transfer several million dollars out of the company's bank account. And where did he wire it? To a bank in the Ukraine, of course.

---

* By the way, never taking vacation is one of the primary indicators that a person is committing fraud. They have to be at work every day to do the things that will allow the fraud to go on undetected. They feel that they can't leave the office for fear that their scheme will fall apart and they will be discovered.

A couple of weeks after his activities were discovered, investigators flew to Kiev and met with representatives of the Ukrainian government, who had been asked to freeze the account containing stolen money. They had frozen it as requested and also seized it. The problem was, they didn't want to give it back. They said that, since it was the proceeds of crime, it belonged to them. The investigators tried to explain to them that this wasn't drug money; it was someone's property. This didn't seem to make a huge amount of difference to the Ukrainians. In the end, political pressure was put on the Ukrainian government and the money, or at least most of it, was returned.

Private Banking

There are people in the world who are so rich, and so out of touch with the lives of ordinary people, that they don't even have the slightest idea of how the world works. They don't know how food mysteriously ends up in the fridge, couldn't tell you the price of a quart of milk or a gallon of gas, and have no idea how

> As a matter of principle, we do not do business with politicians...
> Michael Thomalin,
> *Barclays Private Banking 1998*

to accomplish even the most mundane tasks, like going to the dry cleaners or ordering a pizza or getting cash out of an ATM. So when it comes to their personal finances, it's no surprise that they need a little extra help. And it is precisely for this reason, and for these people, that the concept of private banking was developed. This isn't banking as you and I know it. This is financial management—handholding for the very, very rich.

Never was the rule that "the customer is always right" more strictly applied than in private banking. There's an old joke about this...

A man walks into a private bank and says to the lady employee behind the counter, "I want to open a fucking bank account!"

The lady employee replies, "I beg your pardon?"

The man repeats, "I said, I want to open a fucking bank account!"

The lady employee is shocked and runs for the manager, tells him the story and brings him to the customer.

The manager says to the man, "What seems to be the problem here?"

The man replies, "I have this suitcase with $10 million dollars in it and I want to open a fucking bank account!"

The manager replies, "What? And this bitch won't help you?"

Dictators and warlords, crown princes and prime ministers—everybody needs a bank account and all the other stuff that banks do. But you don't see Baby Doc Duvalier down at the Banque Nationale de Paris, trying to float a loan for a new Prelude. When these people need banking services, the private bankers come to them because these people are willing to pay. They will pay for convenience, but most of all they pay for discretion. Besides, when you're the president of some miserable little African country, where most of your citizens are starving to death, dying of AIDS, or shooting each other, it's bad form to let it slip that the $20 million that the people of the United States gave you last year to buy rice is earning 7.5 percent interest in a Christmas Club account in Liechtenstein.

Correspondent Banking

When banks need to do business in countries where they do not have a physical presence, they often make use of other financial institutions that have facilities there. When a correspondent relationship is established between banks, it means that they can process transactions on each other's behalf. It usually means that one bank's clients can effectively make use of the other bank's services in that country. In most respects, it makes perfect sense and it usually works well. However, there is always a risk. In certain cases, it turns out badly.

It's very much like the argument social agencies put forward to convince people that they should use condoms. They tell them that when they have sex with their partner, they are, in effect, having sex with every person that their partner has slept with. When a bank in North America, for example, enters into a correspondent relationship with a bank in South America, the North American bank is, in reality, doing business with all of the banks and customers that the South American bank has done business with. So unless the bank uses "protection" (as my grandfather used to put it), there's a good possibility that they will get "infected."

In this case, the infection will get into the North American bank's system when it processes funds that originate from an illegal activity such as drug trafficking. The protection would be proper investigative due diligence of the bank they intend to do business with.

If you're a banker and you're approached by a foreign financial institution to enter into a correspondent banking relationship, do yourself a favor and have them thoroughly investigated before you make a move. There are sophisticated investigative firms that will be able to provide you with a profile of the financial institution; they also have local contacts who can give you the inside track on the bank and its senior executives. Doing business without this is like proposing marriage to some chick that you met on the Internet.

Surprisingly, most banks don't do a whole lot of checking before they jump in with both feet. John Mathewson, the former owner of Guardian Bank & Trust in the Cayman Islands who was convicted of money laundering in 1996, maintained correspondent accounts at a number of U.S. banks. Mathewson said that in all the time he ran Guardian, he was never visited even once by a representative of any U.S. bank where he had correspondent accounts.[38]

Don't Deal Dope without It

The world of electronic and online banking has many advantages for criminals, but there are still complications. Suppose you're a marijuana and cocaine trafficker who has been in the business for ten or fifteen years. You've done well for yourself, the evidence of which is that (a) you haven't been caught and (b) you haven't been murdered. Your money is offshore, away from prying eyes and concealed by an impenetrable veil of front companies, all of which were set up years ago by your lawyer in Panama.

But the money isn't much use to you if you can't spend it. And isn't that why you became a drug dealer in the first place? So you could travel around the world, spending the money? You could just start splashing out large amounts of cash, but if you do, you will definitely "heat yourself up." You'd better get a credit card.

Here's how you do it. First you need a lawyer, accountant, private banker or management company. Then you approach a friendly bank in another country that is fairly relaxed about issuing credit cards. If you don't know one, just ask the Panamanian lawyer. What the bank will require is the following:

- A credit card application in your real name.
- A letter from another bank, saying that they know you.

They don't have to say how long they have known you, or where they know you from. They just have to say that they know you.

- A deposit, usually equal to 300 percent of the maximum of the card. So if you want a card with a credit limit of $50,000, you have to supply the bank issuing the card with $150,000.
- A letter from you to the issuing bank, stating that you are not a criminal. There isn't a criminal in the world who wouldn't write that letter!

If you're not that crazy about using your own name all the time, you can also apply at the same time for a supplementary credit card in another name.

Once the bank issues the card, you're set. You can fly around the world, spending as you wish. At the end of each month, the bank that issued the credit card sends the bill to your representative in Panama, who has signing authority on one of your bank accounts. Your representative pays the bill and that's the end of it. You can keep on traveling and spending. Just make sure that when you use the supplementary card in a foreign hotel, you also have a passport with the same name.

This isn't a new idea. In fact, bad guys have been doing this for years and they continue to do it. If you don't feel like giving up the deposit, there are other ways you can trick a bank into issuing a card and becoming your unwitting accomplice. (I won't go into the details of how it can be done.)

Banks that issue cards might want to have a look at the addresses where they are sending credit card statements. If you're the employee assigned this task, don't be surprised if you discover that some statements are being sent to addresses that don't make sense, such as:

- a post office box at a commercial remailing company
- a law firm
- an accounting firm
- a foreign address

The address probably won't be the one the cardholder originally gave to the bank. The bad guys know that credit-recording companies have a pretty sophisticated database that flags most suspicious addresses, for the purpose of detecting fraudulent credit card applications. So at the time of the initial application, the bad guys will often use a legitimate address and then subsequently submit a change of address to the credit card company.

Buddy, Can You Spare a Dinar?

Most of the world's population lives a very hand-to-mouth existence. Many are able to carry their personal net worth around in their pockets or on their back. So it shouldn't surprise you to know that most of them don't have a bank account, either. Not much use in having a bank account if you have nothing to put in it. Besides, they usually spend all of their money on luxuries. Like food.

In places where there are large immigrant populations or a large foreign labor force earning far more than they could at home, you will also find large numbers of currency exchanges (money remitters).* One trait that all immigrants share is the desire to send money to their families back home. They don't earn large salaries, so they're not going to waste it on bank charges.

Take the the Persian Gulf States, for instance. I've been there a bunch of times. I love it. The place is very mysterious and the people

---

* Also called *casa de cambio* or *bureau de change*

are great. Despite what you might hear from CNN, Arabs are definitely the most hospitable people on earth.

The Arabs are doing pretty well. Since they have most of the oil on earth and everyone is lining up to buy it, they have collectively decided that they don't do windows, or any other kind of menial labor, for that matter. So they import foreign workers from Muslim countries, mainly Pakistan and the Philippines. All of these workers send money home. They don't have bank accounts, so they need currency exchanges to do this.

The one in the picture below is in Bahrain. I stood on the street corner for an hour and watched it one Tuesday evening. Forty people went in and did business there during that time. The people back in Pakistan or the Philippines who are receiving the money that is

being sent likely don't have a bank account, either. The money that is being sent to them from these exchanges can be picked up in cash at a bank or at a correspondent exchange in their home country. It's very much cheaper than a bank and just as reliable.

In 1999, I went to Bahrain to put on a course for bankers in money laundering prevention and detection. I told them then that exchange houses were a huge risk for the banks, but they really didn't seem to get what I meant. They couldn't see little exchange dealers as a threat. At the end of the course, I gave them an assignment. They were part of a drug organization and they had to launder a whole bunch of cash and get it to various places in the world. I broke the class into five or six groups and gave them until the next day to come up with a plan. These guys were pretty resourceful and they came up with a number of innovative techniques. But each and every group ended up using currency exchanges are as part of its money laundering process, usually at the placement stage, when they were initially trying to find ways to inject their cash into the banking system.

How do these exchanges get the money to these foreign countries? For the most part, they use banks. So, if you're a bank and you have any money remitters as clients, I have two pieces of bad news for you. The first piece is that these guys are your competitors and you're helping them by providing banking services to them. The second piece of bad news is that you're very probably laundering money as well.

In the developed countries, money remitters are closely monitored by the authorities.

A great number of the currency exchanges in North America are operated by Ismaili Muslims. These people are a specialized sect of the Muslim faith that follows the Aga Khan. They seem to operate two types of businesses: currency exchanges and newsstands. The next time you go into a newsstand in a subway station, have a close look at the place. You may see a photo of the Aga Khan up in between the cigarettes.

These people are pretty honest, in my experience. When I was undercover, I hit on several of them to see if they were interested in taking any dirty money, and they weren't.

Currency exchanges in Western countries typically cater to a particular ethnic population or geographic area. In a Jamaican neighborhood, for example, you will see remitters that specialize in sending money and parcels to Jamaica, and so on. Often you'll see signs in the windows of travel agencies and beauty parlors stating that they will send money overseas for you. These stores are simply acting as agents for larger remitters, and strict enforcement on these businesses by the money laundering cops has been the source of more than one bad hair day down in the 'hood.

His Highness, the Aga Khan

In North America, there is another kind of small currency exchange business that serves the little guy and the bad guy alike. Newspapers and TV are full of advertisements for check cashing services that will lend you money until payday, at a huge rate of interest. As with a currency exchange, you don't need a bank account, you just need to register with them. Often these organizations take unfair advantage of poor people who are on welfare or some other type of social assistance; many such disadvantaged people don't have the luxury of a bank account, so the only place they can go to cash a check is a business that knows them, or to a money remittance/check cashing service.

On the street, there are scores of unscrupulous people who prey on the disadvantaged. Quite often, bars that are frequented by people on welfare will cash welfare or pension checks for the patrons, but they will take as much as 25 percent off the top. If you're an alcoholic or a junkie or a crackhead, it may seem like a good deal.

But buying checks for cash is not only profitable, it's also a great way to get rid of cash in exchange for negotiable instruments that don't cause as much of a problem when you go to deposit them in the bank.

Why Not Buy Your Own Bank?

Sadly, one of the most successful organizations in the history of Mexican business was an illegal one. Known as the Juarez Cartel and reputed to be the world's largest and most successful drug trafficking organization, they were responsible for importing thousands of tons of cocaine and marijuana into the United States.

One of the definitions of organized crime is "a self-perpetuating criminal organization that continues to operate notwithstanding the incarceration or death of any of its members." That description describes the Juarez Cartel perfectly. Until his death in 1997, the leader of the Juarez Cartel was Amado Carillo Fuentes. His nickname, "El Señor de los Cielos," means, roughly, "Lord of the Skies" and was drawn from his penchant for the use of his own aircraft to smuggle cocaine. He owned a couple of aircraft and he made use of them to attain gross revenues that the DEA once estimated at $200 million per week.[39]

In 1993, Carillo was sitting down to dinner in a Mexico City restaurant with a few friends. The Tijuana Cartel, Carillo's main rivals, somehow found out he would be there and sent assassins to kill him. But there was someone else there when the shooting started: Rafael Macedo de la Concha, a.k.a. "El Metro,"* a former Mexican drug cop who had at one time been responsible for interdicting the flow of drugs across the southern border. El Metro saved Carillo's life that night in the restaurant. Within months, he became one of Carillo's top guys. (In fact, in 1997, when Carillo actually did check out, it was El Metro who took over running the cartel.)

Carillo put him in charge of the transshipment of Colombian cocaine through Yucatan, and he was very good at his job. Another thing that El Metro was apparently pretty good at was corrupting local politicians. Although, admittedly, corrupting most Mexican politicians doesn't require huge amounts of effort, El Metro was able to secure the cooperation of Mario Villanueva, the governor of Quintana Roo, a state in the Yucatan peninsula. Allegedly, Villanueva was paid $500,000 every time a big cocaine load successfully made it through the Yucatan and into the U.S. When his time in office ended, everyone had pretty well figured out that he was dirty, so Villanueva got out of Dodge. He avoided capture for a couple of years, but the Mexicans finally got him in May of 2001.

El Metro went into hiding, too. The cops finally caught up with him down in the state of Tabasco (where they make the sauce). He had undergone a lot of plastic surgery to try to change his appearance and he had lost a ton of weight, too! But it didn't help. In 2001, El Metro caught the last train to the U.S. The government of the new Mexican president, Vicente Fox, extradited him to face drug charges.[40] The final irony, though, was that Carillo, having survived countless assassination attempts and gun battles with the law, finally got it in a most unexpected way. The Juarez Cartel seemed to have a

* I tried to find out how "El Metro" earned his nickname, but no one seems to know. My guess is that maybe he was conceived in a subway car.

fixation on plastic surgery, but, lacking the willpower of El Metro, Carillo opted to lose weight by undergoing liposuction. Whoever performed the procedure must have sucked up something that Carillo needed, because he expired on the operating table.

Many believe that Carillo faked his own death. He traveled extensively and had contacts in a large number of countries, including Cuba, where he had a second family. However, the DEA have stated that they have confirmed by fingerprints that Carillo is, in fact, dead. But if those fingerprints were supplied by the Mexican government...who really knows?

The reason I'm telling you all this is the $200 million per week that I mentioned a few pages back. It's a lot of money, and you can't just walk into a bank and deposit it. So what the cartel did was simply buy a bank. That kind of coin allows you to hire very sophisticated people to manage it. The Juarez Cartel's two main money guys were Juan Alberto Zepeda and Jorge Fernando Bastida. In April 1996, on behalf of the cartel, Zepeda and Bastida purchased, for $3.5 million, a holding company called Grupo Corporativo Anahuac. This holding company owned 20 percent of the shares of Banco Anahuac, a Mexico City bank, and 20 percent of the stock meant that the Carillo organization now had a controlling interest in the bank. Once they had that, laundering the cartel's drug money became a lot easier. Foreign banks never questioned transfers from a legitimate financial institution like Banco Anahuac and the cartel's money flowed smoothly.

Meanwhile, back in the USA, the government wasn't exactly asleep. The cartel's control of Banco Anahuac was too big a deal to stay secret for very long. In April 1998, the IRS executed seizure warrants for $3.3 million at five U.S. financial institutions. Warrants were executed at Stanford International Bank, Barnett Bank, the New York office of Bear Stearns and the New York and Miami offices of Republic National Bank.[41] In their affidavit to obtain the warrants,[42] the IRS Criminal Investigation Division alleged that more than $30 million had been moved from Banco Anahuac in Mexico to those five financial institutions.

The transactions were blatantly suspicious, yet, because they were from a "legitimate" financial institution, they were never questioned. Take a look at a few of them and see what you think:

- Mrs. Zepeda opened two accounts at Republic National Bank of Miami. There wasn't much activity for a while; the balance was never more than $75,000 in either account. Then, in April 1997, the accounts became very active. Between April 29 and June 25, $645,000 was wire-transferred into the two accounts. Soon after, four checks, totaling $571,000, were written on the accounts.
- On June 6, 1997, Mr. Zepeda opened an account at Stanford International Bank and transferred $104,000 from his existing account at Bear Stearns. Thirteen days later, he wire-transferred another $400,000 from Bear Stearns. Two weeks after that, he wired $200,000 back to Bear Stearns.
- On June 24, 1997, Mr. Zepeda opened an account at Republic National Bank of New York. Zepeda told the bank that the purpose of the account was to look after his condo fees and bills in Miami. Within three weeks, Zepeda wired or deposited close to $1.2 million into the account. Then he wired $900,000 back out again!

To me, it looks like they were knocking money around from account to account to make it more difficult to track. Clearly, there was a breakdown in vigilance somewhere. For example, when Mr. and Mrs. Zepeda initially established their accounts at Republic, they both used inactive social security numbers to identify themselves.

Bastida deposited $1.19 million into his Stanford account in the form of five checks. All of the checks came from the same Mexican currency exchange house. They all had the same date of issue and the check numbers were consecutive!

To be fair, all of this happened in the late 1990s and the banks have all grown up quite a bit since then, or at least I hope they have. I doubt if this kind of thing would happen today, but what it does show is that even a little bit of due diligence, mixed with some common sense, would have helped.

Clearly, Zepeda and Bastida were able to get as far as they did because of their association with Banco Anahuac. But if you run a bank and decide to rely, sight unseen, on the due diligence of another entity such as a financial institution or a law firm, you should always remember that you are effectively placing your reputation, and possibly your freedom, in their hands. In this case, maybe someone should have asked for their income tax returns. Zepeda had no reported income in 1994, 1995 or 1997; 1996 was a good year, though; he declared $500,000. Bastida had no reported income between 1994 and 1997, even though he was registered as an employee of the Mexican National Electric Company, earning a whopping $15,000 per year.

The Stanford International Bank in Antigua was more than happy to do business with Zepeda and Bastida, believing them to be "businessmen." When they discovered the truth, the Stanford Bank cooperated immediately and the $3 million belonging to the Juarez Cartel was frozen.[43] The moneys were eventually forfeited and the Antiguan government received $1.5 million as their part of an asset-sharing agreement. "Asset sharing" between the U.S. government and other countries is a fairly common occurrence. If a country cooperates with the U.S. government on a money laundering investigation into funds held in that country, then the cooperating nation will receive back a portion of the money seized commensurate with its degree of cooperation.

Anyone doing business with a bank in a drug source country, or any country, for that matter, should ask himself or herself this: if there was a change in the beneficial ownership of a financial institution I was dealing with—that is, if the bank was bought by the biggest drug lord in the hemisphere—would I know it?

Hawallah by any Other Name

Two or three thousand years ago, merchants in India and China developed a system to safely transfer large sums of gold. They called it "hawallah." It is still in use today and it has become a popular and reliable way to move money secretly.

In ancient times, merchants traveled great distances across the Asian continent to trade goods. For example, a merchant traveling from the south to the north of India to buy Chinese silk would be obliged to carry large amounts of gold on the trip. There were bandits everywhere in those days, and the merchants would have to bring along a small army to keep from being waylaid. Even with an armed escort, they often lost their lives and commerce became almost impossible. So the hawallah system was developed, making it safer to travel.

Prior to his journey, a merchant would visit a hawallah dealer and give him the gold he was going to use to buy the silk. The dealer would give the merchant a piece of paper with a symbol on it, usually an animal, because very few people could read or write, and the address of one of his associates in the north. The merchant would then travel to northern India and visit the other hawallah dealer. The dealer in the north would provide, in exchange for the piece of paper bearing the symbol, the same amount of gold to the merchant, less a small percentage, of course. The merchant could then safely go and buy his silk. The various hawallah dealers would settle up with each other from time to time, but since there was lots of trade back and forth, things usually evened out.

The only problem with this system was that there was no way to tell the bandits about it, so they went on killing and robbing merchants for a long time until they figured it out. And even with such an exchange system, they could still rob the merchant of his silk on the trip south. Hawallah, also called *hundi* and several other names, is the most pervasive nonbank financial system in the world. Almost every ethnic group has a similar system, based on a network of relatives, friends and business associates around the world. In most cities, hawalladars (the guys who run the hawallah) advertise in the local ethnic newspapers. By far the largest share of the money moved by these groups is legitimate, and the worst thing that most of them are doing is maybe helping someone avoid tax and foreign currency exchange controls. It would be fairly labor-intensive for a drug trafficking organization to make use of a hawallah system as their primary method of money transfer. Besides, criminals often wish to convert the cash into another financial instrument and most (but not all) hawallahs operate as a cash business at both ends. But hawallah is still used by certain criminal groups and has been encountered frequently by law enforcement agencies around the world, particularly in the U.K., where there is a large South Asian population.

But clearly, the bigger issue is that hawallah and other systems like it are tailor-made for terrorist groups, who need only small amounts of money transferred across national borders to pay for such things as expenses, equipment, false documents, etc.

Forged Documents

Although there are some crime groups that still counterfeit currency, the use of anti-counterfeit measures in currency has greatly reduced

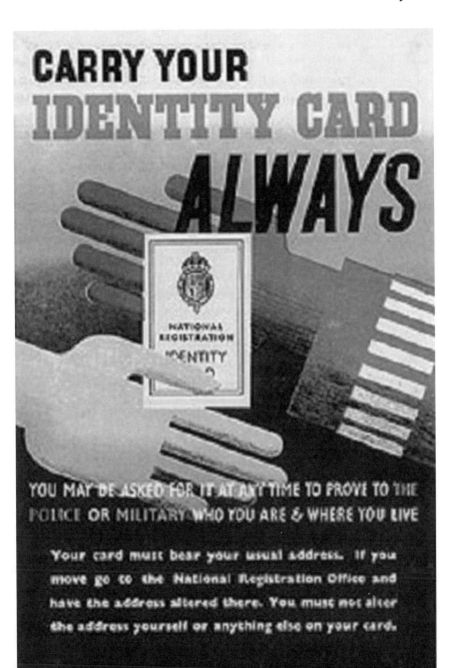

the popularity of this crime. The bad guys finally figured out that it's a bad idea to counterfeit things that people are familiar with...like money. But if you make phony Italian government bonds or passports from Botswana, chances are most people have never seen one.

And with advances in software and hardware, you too can become a forger in the comfort of your own home!

The Organization for Economic Co-operation and Development (OECD), the body that created the FATF, is a group of thirty member countries "sharing a commitment to democratic government and the

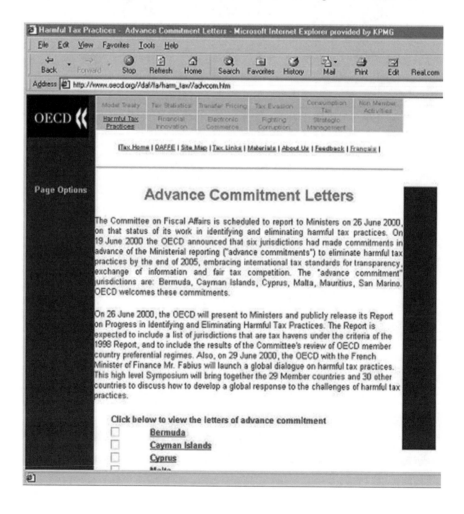

market economy." Based in France, it grew out of the body that administered the Marshall Plan in Europe after World War II. It isn't part of the larger United Nations Organization. They have a website at oecd.org., where you will find all sorts of information about international financial cooperation and tax issues. All pretty boring stuff. But last year I found some interesting stuff on their site. You can see on page 186 the way the site looked last year. They've changed it since then and I'll show you why.

What this site is referring to is an agreement by several countries to participate in a program that will eliminate something called "harmful tax competition." Still bored? Me too, but keep going, it gets better.

Now, all of these countries—Bermuda, Cayman Islands, etc.—sent letters agreeing to cooperate. It must have been a big deal for the OECD, because somebody thought it would be a good idea to post copies of these letters on the website... in JPG format!

On the following page is one from the governor of the Cayman Islands.

The problem with this is that now any enterprising criminal can see what the letterhead of the governor of the Cayman Islands looks like. As well, you can see how his handwriting and his signature appear. And you can download them off the net!

Just for fun, I did exactly that. I isolated the governor's signature and handwriting. And then, using Adobe Photoshop software, I played around with it.

On page 189 is what I was able to cook up on a rainy afternoon. I'm not a professional forger, but to me it looks pretty good. The bad guys that I used to run with—they *live* for stuff like this!

Of course, it isn't only organized crime that makes use of false documents. Here is an interesting excerpt from the testimony of convicted terrorist Ahmed Ressam:

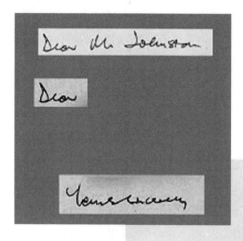

Office of the Governor
Grand Cayman
Cayman Islands

Commitment Letter

May 18, 2000

Mr. Donald J Johnston
OECD Secretary General
Organisation For Economic
Cooperation and Development (OECD)
2, rue Andre Pascal
75775 Paris, CEDEX16
France

I am writing in connection with OECD's project on harmful tax competition. I am pleased to inform you that the Cayman Islands hereby commits to the elimination of tax practices determined by the Forum to be harmful in accordance with the OECD's Report, *"Harmful Tax Competition: An Emerging Global Issue"* (the OECD Report). In fulfilment of this commitment, the Cayman Islands undertakes to implement such measures (including through any legislative changes) as are necessary for the elimination of those aspects of the Cayman Islands regimes deemed to be harmful. The Government of the Cayman Islands commits in particular to a programme of effective exchange of information in tax matters, transparency, and the elimination of any aspects of the regimes for financial and other services that attract business with no substantial domestic activities. Measures designed to eliminate the tax practices deemed to be harmful are broadly outlined in the attachment hereto. Details of these measures and a specific timetable will be agreed with the Forum. We understand that the OECD is prepared to assist us in establishing, improving, or maintaining such practices and procedures as are necessary to comply with this commitment.

The Government of the Cayman Islands further commits to refrain from:

(1) introducing any new regime that would constitute a harmful tax practice under the OECD Report;

(2) for any existing regime related to financial and other services that currently does not constitute a harmful tax practice under the OECD Report, modifying the regime in such a way that, after modifications, it would constitute a harmful tax practice under the OECD Report; and

(3) strengthening or extending the scope of any existing measure that currently constitutes a harmful tax practice under the OECD Report.

CAYMAN ISLANDS
Office of the Governor
Grand Cayman
Cayman Islands

May 12, 2001

Mr. W. Christopher Mathers
Box 448 GT
298 Spinnaker Drive
Grand Cayman

Dear Mr Mathers

I am pleased to inform you that upon the advice of the Minister of Immigration, the Government of the Cayman Islands hereby grants you Citizenship and Permanent Residency as defined by Section 14(2)(a) of the *Immigration and Citizenship Act of the Cayman Islands {1995}*.

Your status is in force as of this date and you may, at your convenience submit your application for a Cayman Islands passport to the Passport Control Office.

The formal Citizenship Court will take place on Wednesday, the seventh day of June, 2001, at 5:30 in the afternoon at the Governor's Residence.

Please accept my congratulations and I look forward to seeing you again at that time.

P J SMITH
GOVERNOR

The Government of the Cayman Islands intends to release this letter of commitment to the public and would welcome the OECD's release of this letter after the Committee of Fiscal Affairs reports to the OECD Council on the progress of its work, which we understand is expected by mid-June 2000.

P J SMITH
GOVERNOR

Q. What country did you see Abu Zubeida* in?

A. In Pakistan.

Q. He was leader of the camps?

A. Yes.

Q. Did you discuss anything when you met with Abu Zubeida on your return back to Canada?

A. Yes. He asked me to send him some passports, some original passports, if I had, that he can use to give to other people who had come to carry out operations in U.S.

Q. What type of passports was he looking for?

A. Canadian passports, but original.

Q. Did he tell you the names of the people he wanted those passports for?

A. He gave me some of the names.

Counterfeit Passports

Counterfeit ID is invaluable to money launderers. Even if the quality of work will not withstand the scrutiny of a customs or immigration officer, a bad guy may still be able to use it to open a bank account or get a driver's license. Unfortunately, bank employees aren't as vigilant as they could be about such things. And while you can't expect every teller to become as proficient as the experts at detecting fraudulent documents, there are some relatively simple ways to give a document a quick examination.

On page 192 is an example of a forged passport. (On the street, a forged passport is called a "book.") You will notice a number of telltale signs that are common in all kinds of forged documents, including passports, such as:

* Abu Zubeida was an al Qaeda member and one of Osama bin Laden's lieutenants.

- "sawtooth" cuts in the laminate corners
- double thickness of plastic laminate on the photo page
- missing pages
- restitching of the spine
- air bubbles in the laminate
- glue smears
- hand-drawn security features

You can see in this passport where the photo has been replaced and then the seals have been hand-drawn. In fact, this forgery has almost all of the telltale signs of a forgery.

You've probably noticed that when you go through Immigration control at the airport, the officer will often put your passport under a small ultraviolet light (page 192, bottom). You'll notice that under a UV light, the hand-drawn seals are quite apparent and in no way resemble what the real thing should look like.

There are a number of sites on the Internet where you can purchase documents that will identify you as anything from a bail bondsman to a foreign diplomat. They aren't a whole lot of good in Europe or North America, but you might be able to get by on them in the Third World.

You can also buy false documents for your own protection. This isn't illegal. There are a couple of companies on the net that sell "camouflage passports." These are passports for countries that no longer exist, such as Burma, Rhodesia and British Honduras, to name just three. They are not intended to be used to enter a country, although I am confident that plenty of Third World immigration officers don't know that British Honduras is now Belize. Their purpose is purportedly for foreign travelers, particularly Israeli or U.S. citizens, who would become targets in the event of a hijacking or a hostage-taking. In most terrorist hostage-takings, the bad guys collect the passports of all of the hostages to see who

Passport, as seen under ultraviolet light.

and what they have. Depending on who's taking the hostages, you may not want them to know that you're an American or an Israeli. The idea is that, when asked to provide your passport, you give them the camouflage one and you won't be targeted. They are pretty realistic-looking, and they even come with exit and entry stamps from countries the bearer has supposedly visited.

If terrorists jack you and you have the presence of mind to give up your camouflage passport, you'll probably survive: the schools these guys went to aren't big on geography. Instead, they learn all about how martyrs and suicide bombers go to heaven and are greeted by forty virgins (some say the number is seventy-two) who will service their every whim.*

---

* This is something that I find confusing. Instead of virgins, if you had a choice, wouldn't you ask for chicks with experience?

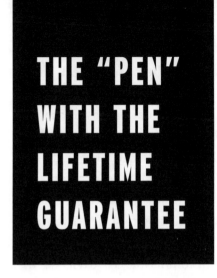

THE "PEN" WITH THE LIFETIME GUARANTEE

The most anxious man in a prison is the warden.

GEORGE BERNARD SHAW
(1856–1950)

So You're Going to Prison!

These days, a lot of people are going to prison who never, ever thought that they would. Board members, executives and auditors have been discovering, more and more, lately, that what they thought were smart business practices are, in fact, what the rest of us refer to as fraud.

How did all of this unethical behavior end up happening? If it's true, and I believe that it is, that the vast majority of business people are honest and ethical, how do they end up getting into trouble?

It's just like everything else; you just sort of slide into it. Imagine a scenario like this. Steve is the CEO of a medium-size, publicly traded company that manufactures electronic components for aircraft navigation systems. Their stock was relatively stable through the 1990s but recently, 9/11 and the related slowdowns in the aviation industry hit Steve's company pretty hard. The stock has lost almost 75 percent of its value in the past six months and Steve is up against it. Steve is an honest man. He pays his taxes and has always prided himself on the ethical behavior of the company and its employees.

Les is Steve's auditor. He too is an honest, ethical family man. Over the years, Les's small independent accounting firm has grown along with, and mainly on account of, the success of Steve's company. Les and Steve have been friends for many years. They and their wives socialize constantly and their two families holiday together every year.

One November, Steve and Les meet for their usual weekly lunch. Steve complains to Les that business is bad. Orders he had hoped to receive simply have not come in. The last quarter was dismal and this one isn't looking better. Steve tells Les that things are so bad that he may have to lay people off, and it's almost Christmas. The employees are like family to Steve. Giving them jobs is the only way he can really measure his success. He confesses to Les that he has been losing sleep and that his health is starting to suffer. Two nights ago, he had chest pains.

Les tries to allay Steve's worries but to no avail. Steve tells Les that he has an idea. They have a substantial order confirmed for the next quarter from a French aircraft manufacturer. A U.S. commuter airline has ordered sixteen planes from them and Steve's firm will supply the navigation electronics, starting in February. Steve tells Les that if they were to record half of those sales on the books in this quarter, he could keep things afloat and he wouldn't have to lay anyone off.

"Technically," of course, that would be wrong, Les tells Steve. But because of the personal relationship that they have, Les feels that he has no choice. They go ahead with it and nobody is laid off for Christmas.

In January, the French government decides that they will not support U.S. military initiatives in the Middle East. A patriotic furor erupts and French products are boycotted. All over the United States, people stop buying bottled water, smelly cheese and over-priced wine.

The commuter airline immediately cancels its order for the French aircraft. Steve's company loses the big February order. But, guess what, it's already on the books. Now Steve has to borrow from another future order to cover off the loss. And so on and so on, until, finally, Les has to do the right thing. The company declares bankruptcy; Steve and Les get done by the SEC for fraud. Everyone loses their job. Steve and Les are arrested, tried and convicted.

And that is how it happens. People don't always set out to commit crimes. Sometimes, good people, honest people, just get on that continuum of criminality by doing a small thing and end up doing a big thing.

At Least It's a North American Institution

If you're going to commit a crime, my suggestion to you is that you try to do it in a democracy. At least in a democracy, you have a chance of beating the rap. A couple of years ago, I was in Saudi Arabia, making a speech on money laundering to some very serious banker types. When I told them that, in Canada, prisoners were allowed to vote in federal elections, they laughed at me and asked me what I had been smoking. But I pressed on and finally convinced them that it was true. Strangely enough, inmates seem to vote very conservatively, too! They actually believe in law and order, and the death penalty... as long as it's not them that's getting it, of course.

What's more, they can also use the telephone in there! And if you think about it, maybe it's not a bad idea that they let them use the phone. After all, should incarceration be an impediment to the continuing operation of your drug trafficking business? The Correctional Service of Canada doesn't seem to think so.

From time to time, the police will intercept the private communications of prisoners by tapping the pay phones or by bugging their cells or the visiting rooms. You usually don't get a whole lot of intelligence from these kinds of intercepts, but once in a while, you do. And just to show you how things are, here's a short transcript from an intercept that was made in the early 1990s. The inmate is a Russian criminal, locked up in Kingston Penitentiary, in Canada. He is calling his friend, presumably another criminal, in St. Petersburg, in the former Soviet Union.

Inmate: I'm in prison in Canada and I eat meat three times a day.
Friend: Meat?
Inmate: Yes. And potatoes…you should come here and commit a crime.

What to Expect on the Inside

In the event of a fraudulent accounting or money laundering scandal, it's the most senior executives that are going to be pulling the time. It's true that they may not pull a huge amount of time, but they still have to do it. And anyone who says that doing time, even short time,* is easy, has obviously never done any.

When you're convicted of a serious crime, there are certain things that happen to you, no matter what country you're in. For the moment, though, I'll leave out less enlightened countries like Saudi Arabia or Vietnam where the penal system is still set up to actually serve as a deterrent.

It's no wonder bad guys the world over want to get arrested in Canada. If your life isn't going all that well and you don't have anywhere else to go, you might want to consider pulling some federal time there.

Here are just a few of the many benefits of a Canadian prison sentence. One, free sex-change operations: the Canadian courts have ordered that the Correctional Service must pay for surgical procedures for male inmates who feel that they are women trapped in a man's body. These operations don't happen all at once, either. There is a stage where the inmate has all of the exterior female features but

* Although it varies from place to place, "short time" usually refers to less than five years in prison.

still has his male parts "under the hood." Believe me, a male prisoner with breasts is always a popular guest at prison parties. Two, more chances to go over the wall (escape). That's assuming that there *is* a wall; one inmate at a minimum-security joint called a taxi from inside the prison and then just waited for it at the gate. If you think that's bizarre, here's another one: the courts said it was acceptable for a con (convict; inmate) to bring an action against the Correctional Service because they woke him up in the middle of the night to do a head count. Apparently this caused him dizziness and neurological damage. And, finally, just in case you happen to be both a criminal and a warlock, the Correctional Service will provide a Wiccan priest so you can practice your religion.[44]

After the Verdict and Sentencing

You may find yourself sitting around in a local lockup for a day to two, waiting for transport. In the U.S., a money laundering offense or other financial crime is usually a federal "beef" (criminal charge), and if you are convicted, the U.S. Marshals will escort you to a prison facility. In Canada, if your sentence is greater than two years, you will be sent to a federal prison facility.

In either case, upon arriving at the facility you will be sequestered and searched. One of the big concerns of correctional services in every country is the smuggling and distribution of "contraband" inside the institutions. Contraband can be anything but usually refers to narcotics or items of value, usually cash. Since every con knows he is going to be strip-searched, there are traditionally two methods employed to smuggle contraband on your person. The first one, "swallowing," is exactly what it sounds like: swallowing the contraband, usually wrapped in condoms, and then recovering it after it passes through your system.

This is also a popular method of concealment employed by drug couriers. Over the years, I worked a number of cases where couriers smuggled narcotics by swallowing them, wrapped in condoms or plastic wrap. Couriers take anti-diarrhea pills to keep themselves from passing them on the plane home. Each pellet is encased in one condom inside another. The ends are tied off with dental floss and then the excess trimmed. They are doubled so that, in case the courier does pass them, he or she can simply peel off the first condom, rinse the pellet, and swallow it again.

Some city cop friends of mine had an informant who was a very active courier and regularly traveled to Jamaica, where he would swallow as many as thirty condoms of hashish oil at one time. One night, they saw him getting off a flight from Jamaica and followed him from the airport. He took a cab to a hotel and then realized that he had no money. They watched in disbelief as he dropped his pants in the back seat of the cab and popped out a condom, which he cleaned up and gave to the cabbie as payment for the fare.

Police at most international airports have a "dry cell." This is a cell without a flush toilet, only a chair with a hole in the seat and a bucket underneath. Drug couriers are left there until the moment of truth, and then the condoms are collected. How long can a person hold out? A drug courier in Sweden held out for twenty-two days. He finally let go while he was asleep.

Swallowing condoms of hash or hashish oil is risky, and if the condoms break in the courier's stomach, he or she can become very ill. But smuggling heroin or cocaine in this fashion is far more dangerous. In the early 1980s, I was involved in a case that demonstrated just how true that is. Sammy was a Lebanese heroin trafficker who was arrested by the Mounties in Ottawa. His co-accused, who I think was his stepfather, fled Canada for Lebanon. Sammy went to prison, but his mother over in Lebanon, like any other mom, wanted to visit her son.

On the flight from Beirut to Montreal, Sammy's mom complained to the flight attendants that she was sick and that she was experiencing stomach pains. In Montreal, she transferred to the one-hour flight to Ottawa. She collapsed on the flight and was DOA when they landed. When they did a post-mortem, they found 105 condoms in her stomach, each containing between three and four grams of heroin, a few of which had ruptured. Apparently the stepfather had told her that if she wanted to visit her son in Canada, she had to pay for her trip by smuggling dope.

There was another case, although I wasn't involved with it, in which a cocaine swallower, realizing that the condoms he had swallowed were leaking or breaking, since he was starting to get high, went into the airport bathroom and performed some do-it-yourself surgery, cutting his own stomach open. When the cops found him, he had successfully removed a number of the condoms, some of which had indeed broken.

But I digress. The second method of smuggling contraband into prison is called "suitcasing." This simply involves inserting the contraband into the rectum. I've never been able to find out exactly why this activity is called suitcasing except for the obvious fact that there is a lot of "packing" required.

The prison systems are full of stories of amazing feats of suitcasing, but I won't go into them here since you wouldn't believe them anyway. It's enough to say that the human body is an amazing machine and is capable of being manipulated in ways that you never dreamed possible. Remember when you were a kid and your mom would always tell you not to put money in your mouth? Well, that's why!

Sizing You Up

The next step in your introduction to life behind bars is "classifica-tion." What this means is that, after they've searched you, the corrections people will decide whether you are high risk, i.e. if you have debts to other inmates, or are HIV positive, an informant, a sex offender, an ex-cop, an ex-judge or an escape risk. Not many guys who pull time for financial crimes fall into any of these categories, and so they end up in the general population. If they're lucky, they end up in a minimum-security institution.*

Prison is a culture all to its own. It can be a very dangerous place for the newcomer. Most guys serving time have been there before and have worked their way up through the prison system, usually starting with time as a juvenile, so they have experience and they know the rules. I could never even begin to provide you with all of the rules here, but I'll tell you some, just to give you a flavor of the place.

When you first arrive, there will be plenty of guys offering to help you out. They'll appear friendly, but they will definitely have their own agenda. In prison, everything is a commodity: drugs, money, even people. The best thing to do is keep to yourself until you figure out what's what. If you're a wealthy guy and your defense lawyer is worth his salt, arrangements can be made to have you protected. In return for a regular payment to their families on the outside, you can hire a couple of "minders" to keep you out of harm's way. You should always hire at least two, because there are twenty-four hours in a day and you don't want any gaps. And if one of them gets paroled or incapacitated, you'll have backup.

You may wonder why a so-called white-collar criminal would need protection. What would an inmate have to gain from hurting

---

* Also referred to as a "farm" or a "camp."

you? The answer is, money. Prisons are all about extortion and violence. I was involved in a case where a mid-level employee of a company stole about $10 million from his employer. All but about $3 million was recovered, and we concluded that he'd spent it; however, the other inmates in the minimum-security institution he was sent to figured that he might still have a bunch of money, so they told him that if he didn't give it up, they would hurt him. Trouble was, he couldn't give it up because he didn't have it. So they tortured him. He showed us cigarette burns all over his body from their attempts to get at the truth. The other method was to threaten him with homosexual rape. We never really asked him how that turned out.

The College of Criminal Knowledge

Some people say that, when you go to prison, it's best not to tell anyone why you are there, but that advice is generally reserved for skinners.* If you are doing time for fraud or money laundering in a prison where there are other inmates who have been convicted of financial crime or are doing time on drug charges, it's usually common knowledge who's in for what. And guys who have been taken off (arrested)** in complex undercover operations will frequently share their knowledge with the other inmates. So prison can be a great place to get an education and make new connections for your later life on the outside. And if you learned about business crime while you were inside, I guess you could call it a "joint" MBA!

The subjects discussed in your "seminars" will be things like

---

* A "skinner," or somebody doing time for a "skin beef," refers to an inmate convicted of a sex crime. They are considered to be just above informants on the prison hierarchical structure.
** To be "taken off" can also mean to be robbed or mugged.

police techniques, failed methods of concealment or the performance of your new friends' defense lawyers—who, incidentally, couldn't have been that good considering that they're doing a stretch (prison sentence). But, human nature being what it is, most guys are reluctant to admit that they were gullible enough to be taken in by an undercover operator, and they often embellish the stories of their particular cases to make themselves seem less dumb. What's hilarious in this is that the bad guys will frequently attempt to convince their fellow prisoners that only ultra-sophisticated police techniques and space-age technology were sufficient to capture such masterminds as themselves, thus making the police out to have capabilities that they clearly don't have.

The result is the perpetuation of a number of criminal "urban myths," stories that the crooks actually believe to be true. For example, I knew of this one dope guy, down on the border, who wouldn't run* drugs on a sunny day. He had heard that the cops were using satellite technology and would be able to track his activities from space, so he always waited for cloud cover before making a move. I suspect the fact that he had his "head in the bag"** most days likely contributed to his suspicious nature.

Prison movies talk about "cells" and "cell-blocks." In most prisons, the inmates refer to their cell as their "house" and the cell-block as a "range." As in any community, there are often disagreements on the range: commercial disputes, lovers' quarrels and political machinations. These disagreements often lead to violence. But if an inmate decides he is going to take action against another inmate on the range, there are—again, as in every society—protocols and procedures that must be respected. The most important of these is that

---

* To "run" drugs means to transport them a long distance, usually across an international border.
** Having your "head in the bag" refers to the use of drugs, usually cocaine.

you must make it known to the rest of the inmates on the range, except the intended victim, of course, that there is going to be a significant event. The reason for this is a simple one. The other prisoners need to know in advance that violence is planned, because once it has taken place, the range will be subjected to a "lock-down,"* and correctional officers, and possibly the police, will search some or all of the cells looking for evidence. Since many of the inmates will have items of contraband secreted in their cells, they expect a warning if there is going to be a search. If they don't get it, they will lose their contraband and possibly be subjected to disciplinary action. If a search happens as a result of something you did, and you don't let anyone know in advance, you will definitely be putting yourself in harm's way.

Even experienced criminals can run into trouble if they don't know the rules in their new environment. About twenty years ago I knew a bad guy I'll call Gavin. Gavin was a very unpleasant person. He was what my mother would call a "bad seed." Gavin liked to hurt people and he was very good at it. I once sat in on a trial where Gavin was charged with assault. He had gone to a bar that was frequented mostly by college kids and decided to do a little light stealing. As he was reaching into some young girl's purse to steal her wallet, her boyfriend, a nice kid from the university who had no experience with people like Gavin, confronted him.

Gavin smashed a beer bottle into the kid's face, several times. He cut him for about a hundred stitches. At the trial, the prosecution and the defense went on for hours about Gavin's "intent." The prosecution contended that Gavin picked up the beer bottle with the intent of smashing it into the kid's face. The defense countered with

---

* Although there are varying degrees of "lock-downs," it normally means that the range or the entire institution is closed. There will be no normal activities such as work, recreation or visits. Inmates are restricted to their cells.

the argument that Gavin simply had the bottle in his hand when he was confronted, possibly even shoved, by the kid. He hadn't picked up the bottle with the intent of hitting the kid, he just happened to have the bottle in the hand that he was hitting the kid with. This argument went on for some time. Finally the judge had heard enough. He sentenced Gavin to three years, partly because of the severity of the injuries and partly because of his twenty or thirty previous convictions.

Gavin had never been to prison; only jails and regional lockups. But he was a very tough guy. He was big, strong and highly motivated.

In prison, meals are served cafeteria style. The inmates line up in an orderly fashion, collect their food and then sit, usually in the same spot every time. On his second day in, six-foot-two Gavin walked up to the line and butted in front of another inmate, a five-foot-three Frenchman who was serving twenty-five years for bank robbery and murder. The Frenchman told him to go to the rear of the line. Gavin responded by telling him to fuck off and, for good measure, calling him a "goof." There were two things that Gavin likely didn't know. The first thing was that calling someone a goof was a huge insult in that particular prison. Second, even Gavin would likely have chosen to say something else had he known that those were to be his last words on earth. The Frenchman pulled out a home-made knife and cut Gavin's throat, right there in the food line. Gavin pumped out (bled to death) in minutes and was gone. Believe me when I say that the world is a better place without him.

COPS, CASH AND CORRUPTION

You are thought here to be the most senseless and fit man for the constable of the watch; therefore bear you the lantern.
Much Ado about Nothing
WILLIAM SHAKESPEARE
(1564–1616)

It Isn't Money, It's Evidence

During my undercover days, my colleagues and I often had literally millions of dollars in cash on the table at any given time. We were always getting money from drug traffickers, and sometimes it was difficult keeping track of what was going on. The obvious danger in a situation like that is that somebody is going to try and steal it—either the bad guys or maybe even one of the cops.

My personal rule was that I always told the bad guys that I didn't want any money to be brought to my office. The last thing we needed was for somebody to come through the front door with a machinegun, trying to shoot up the place; getting shot was not in my job description. Not only that, but the rest of the offices on our floor were occupied by civilians and getting shot wasn't in their job description, either. So we usually met the crooks in hotel lobbies, train stations and airports, and got them to bring us the cash in suitcases. The reason we chose those places was that they are the only places where you can haul around a suitcase and not look suspicious.

During an operation called "Green Ice," some DEA friends of mine almost ended up in a shootout during a money pickup at Orange County airport. As they were doing the pickup, three or four bad guys with police raid-jackets, guns and handcuffs showed up, posing as cops. The crooks didn't know that the pickup guys they were ambushing were DEA undercover agents; they thought that they were money brokers and they were going to "arrest" them, rob them and quite likely murder them. Anyway, that didn't happen and I'm happy to say that no good guys got killed that day.

For some people, though, the problem with a job like this is that they can't quite get over the novelty of handling huge amounts of cash. Sometimes one of the younger guys would hold up a big stack of money and say something like "I could pay off my house with this." I found that kind of talk troubling and I told them so. I told them that it wasn't money, it was evidence, and it had to be treated like evidence. You should never start equating amounts of seized money to actual things. Sometimes people do succumb to the temptation—not as often as you might think, but it happens. Some years ago, several members of the "Majors," a specialized section of the Los Angeles Sheriff's Department that did big drug money cases, were found to be stealing money from seizures, sometimes as much as $100,000 at a time.[45]

The popular PBS news show *Frontline* covered the story in 1990. Several of the indicted members of the Majors were interviewed, including Deputy Dan Garner. There were some interesting points in his account of the way his people dealt with large cash seizures. He said that when the Majors made a large seizure, the counts were always off, that there was always a discrepancy "due to the large volume of notes." In 1987 and 1988, the LASD seized $26 million and $33 million, respectively, from drug traffickers and money couriers.[46]

I worked these kinds of cases for years, and I can tell you that this is baloney. I don't care if you have to count the money ten times, there can't be any discrepancies. In all of my years doing this, I only experienced a shortage once. We had been laundering money for a Caribbean drug dealer named Guy. Guy never knew exactly how much he was giving up; he always relied on us to give him a count afterwards. This is pretty common among dope dealers, in my experience. Possibly because many of them just can't count, but probably because they are traveling around from one stash house to the next and they just don't have the time or the patience to count the cash. Our guys did a pickup from Guy that day and brought it back to be counted. After the count, I called him and told him that the total was $50,000. A week or so later, we discovered that we were short; I think it was about $13,000. Granted, this wasn't a big amount in the scheme of things—we handled millions of dollars—but it was serious. Everyone was concerned that someone had crossed the line.

After a lengthy inquiry, our people finally figured out that my guys had simply done a miscount of the bundles; that they had counted some stacks of $20 notes as fifties. We had a newcomer working with us that day, a very pretty girl. I think that maybe the guys were a bit distracted.

But I was the one who had to go back to Guy and tell him that his $50,000 had somehow shrunk to $37,000. Oh well, I guess that's why they were paying me the not-so-big bucks.

Guy took the news surprisingly well. Part of the reason, I think, was that Guy was under the impression that my partners and I had been making him huge profits in the stock market. Prior to being introduced to us, it would have been a safe bet that Guy wasn't reading the *Wall Street Journal*. But once we started "investing" his money for him, I had some fun by pointing out stocks that had made huge price jumps and then telling Guy that we had bought him a bunch of it just before the price went up. On one occasion, he came to the office in a panic. He had seen in the paper that morning that one of the stocks we had told him he owned had suffered a horrific drop in price. I told him to relax, that we knew about the impending price drop and we'd sold his position the previous day. He was so relieved!

Guy was finally arrested and convicted of all sorts of drug offenses. But, in the end, the thing that really hurt Guy wasn't so much the conviction as the story of his arrest as it was told in court.

Turned out that Guy was very nervous for a drug dealer, and on one occasion, when he realized that he was under police surveillance, he had thrown up from anxiety. This anecdote didn't do anything to bolster Guy's reputation as a bad-ass. The mortifying revelation occurred whilst the prisoners' box was jammed to the boards with many of his fellow miscreants, who, to a man, all seemed to enjoy the sense of Schadenfreude* that is so often elusive when one is facing the prospect of several years in the can.

Like everything else, the lapse at the L.A. sheriff's office was the result of a bunch of factors. First, a lack of training. People who work in positions of trust often need integrity training; that is to say, some people don't know the difference between right and wrong. They need to be taught. Sociologist Emile Durkheim said that in any society, there will be a percentage of deviants. The trick is to keep those deviants away from jobs where they will be handling a million dollars in cash every day. But what if it's "good" cops that take the money? Cops with good records, family men, previously honest men. How does it happen? The answer is that it's the same old "continuum of crime" thing.

Lots of departments used to effect seizures from traffickers and not even bother indicting them. They would stop a stash car with a million dollars in it and have the occupants sign a waiver saying that they had no claim to the money. The problem with this is that there are no court proceedings, and no strict requirement for continuity of evidence. This is a police rule based on the legal concept of "continuity of possession." What this means is that every time a piece of evidence is transferred from one person to another, there has to be a record of where, when and why it was moved. This is particularly

---

* A German word that simply means "experiencing pleasure from the misfortune of another." I had been searching for a way to use this word in the book as it is quite popular among journalists and intellectuals, of which I am neither.

important in cases where there is a danger of tainting the evidence. In a drug case, the suspected narcotics need to be analyzed by a government scientist who will provide a certificate of analysis that they are, in fact, narcotics. In a murder case, when DNA that may belong to the suspect is recovered from the victim (vaginal swabs, fingernail scrapings, etc.), it is important that the prosecution can account for the whereabouts of the sample at all times, from the moment it was seized from the victim until it ended up in the crime lab under a microscope. Without this kind of procedural strictness, there is more opportunity for sloppy record keeping and theft.

In the case of the L.A. Sheriff's Department, the bosses were putting pressure on the Majors for more seizures, and they did make more seizures, but unfortunately they used the fact that they were busy as an excuse for sloppy work.

Another consideration is more political. Should police agencies be able to keep the money they seize? And, if so, is it correct to tie police budgets to seizures?

In my experience, this kind of thing is fraught with problems. The minute a police agency begins to retain seized money, their political masters will start slashing their existing budgets. In places like the City of Los Angeles, the municipal administration actually put cash seizures down as part of the police budget. To be on budget, the LAPD were *required* to maintain a threshold level of cash seizures. The police department had to find money; it had become a profit center, another source of revenue for the city.

This isn't a problem as long as the cash seizures keep coming in, but what happens when times change? What happens when the guys have worked a big case and then half of them spend the following year in court and not out on the street seizing more money?

What happens is that there's less money for things like gas, training, equipment, vehicle maintenance. What happens is that police administrators end up under the gun. As you might expect, they apply pressure on the unit commanders, who, in turn, put the squeeze on the investigators to effect more money seizures. But policing is not supposed to be about seizing cash from drug traffickers. It's about serving and protecting the population. Plus, what kind of traffickers are they going to target? Answer: the ones that are the easiest to catch and seize money from. What this means is that the sophisticated traffickers, who have successfully concealed the beneficial ownership of their assets and aren't easy pickings for a "quick hit" money seizure, aren't going to be targeted.

This is not usually an issue for federal law enforcement agencies. Unlike many regional and local law enforcement departments, federal agencies turn any seized proceeds of crime over to the government. It's a lot easier to ask them for a budget increase than it is to depend on seizures. Especially if you are sending them a check several times a year.

As a footnote, you should know that I worked with the Narcotics Division of the L.A. Sheriff's Department and I have no complaints. I found them to be a professional and dedicated group of men and women. They have a horribly difficult job, enforcing the law in a city that has more dope than Bogotá and more guns than Beirut.

One Million Ways to Get into Trouble?

I remember on one occasion a dope-dealing ex-cop had his people drop off a suitcase with about a million dollars in it. He called me and said, "I'm not sure how much is there, but I know it's at least a million." I told him that, just from looking, I figured it was about $1,100,000. But when we finally counted it, it was $1,037,000. I called the guy back and told him the lesser amount and he said,

> I generally avoid temptation, unless I can't resist it.
> MAE WEST
> (1893–1980)

"The Colombians need a million this time; just put the $37,000 against the next one." And that was it. No muss, no fuss, whatever I said was fine with him. The point is that, as a cop, the best year I ever had, I may have made $77,000 in salary. If there had really been $1.1 million that day, I could have stolen $63,000 and no one would have been the wiser. And that's the problem with this kind of work. There are plenty of opportunities to steal and never be found out. The opportunity for corruption is enormous.

As well, other cops, particularly the older ones, never seemed to have a grasp on exactly what it was that we undercover guys were doing. One day, this old dope cop comes to me and says that he and his squad are heading to Aruba to "flash"* some money for some dope. He gave me about $600,000 Canadian and asked me to get him U.S. dollars. If you think Canadian money isn't worth that much in Canada, try taking it out of the country. No self-respecting dope dealer would ever take it. The boys needed real money, so I did the foreign exchange transaction for them.

About six weeks later, the old dope cop calls me up and tells me that they busted the bad guys in Aruba and now he needs to convert the U.S. dollars back into Canadian "dollarettes." During the time that the boys were down in Aruba getting a tan, the value of the Canadian dollar had slipped even lower, if that's possible. So when I changed the money back for them, they ended up with about $15,000 extra. When I tried to give the $615,000 to the old dope cop, he wouldn't take the fifteen. He told me, "I gave you six hundred grand and that's what I want back." I tried to explain to him that what he had done essentially was take a foreign exchange "position." He wasn't having any of that. I eventually ended up

---

* "Flashing" means showing a large amount of money, called a "flashroll," to drug traffickers. The flashroll money is never intended to be given up to the bad guys; you just use it to get them to produce the dope so you can bust them.

calling someone in finance and cutting them a check for the extra.

The point of this story is that I could have kept the difference; no one would have even thought to check the change of interest rates. As well, we were exchanging Canadian for U.S. dollars every day for a variety of crooks. It would have been a simple thing to sell the crooks the U.S. dollars from the Aruba thing and give the cops back the dopers' Canadian money. I could have gotten in the middle of those two transactions, made myself another $50,000, and no one would have been the wiser.

Obviously, I didn't do it. But the problem is that if you are in this environment for an extended period of time and you have certain flaws in your character, or you are in a financial bind, you might slip.

The overwhelming danger to law enforcement officers who are involved in these types of cases is the rationalization of criminal behavior. Most cops who steal money (and don't go thinking that there's a lot of them, because there aren't) are able to come up with what they consider to be a good reason to take the money. Here's the logic:

> This is drug money.
> It comes from bad people who do very bad things with it.
> If I take this money, I will use it to buy a bigger house, in a nice neighborhood.
> I will use it to send my child to a private school.
> My child will be well adjusted and happy because of the things that this money will do for him.
> Because he's so well adjusted and happy, he will excel in school and go on to university.
> The money will help pay for his education at a good school, where he will go on to become a doctor.
> As a doctor, he will find the cure for cancer.
> Thousands of lives will be saved.
> So I am going to take the money.

It sounds crazy, I'll admit, but I'm convinced that it's true. Cops who steal money typically end up living visibly beyond their means—buying the big house, sending their kids to private schools. And they nearly always get caught.

ECONOMIC SUBVERSION AND THE GRAY MARKET ECONOMY

Everyone knows why cash deals are common: you can escape the scrutiny of the tax man. Some small businesses and tradesmen operate on a cash-only basis for that reason, and in countries where you pay a tax on goods and services, like Canada, their customers are often happy to oblige, because it means they too can avoid paying that little bit extra. However, there's another advantage to cash transactions or cash-only businesses. They're ideal structures for laundering money.

One Hour Later, You'll Feel Like Laundering Money Again!

If you go to Chinatown in any large city in North America, you'll notice that many of the businesses don't take credit cards. This hasn't always been the case. Chinese business people used to be happy to accept credit cards. They didn't want to keep cash on the premises because of the number of violent armed robberies and shootings that were prevalent within the Asian community. However, all that decreased markedly in the early 1990s when a number of "one-man crime waves" were either locked up by the police, deported as illegal immigrants or murdered by their colleagues.

Many of them operate on a cash-only basis now. There are two reasons for this. One is that over the last ten years, Asian organized crime groups have learned that they can make a lot more money doing credit card frauds than violent crimes. There's less chance that they'll be caught, the jail terms are shorter, and last but not least, the likelihood of getting shot is significantly lower as well. And it's a lot easier to pull off a substantial credit card fraud if you have a cooperating merchant. This being the case, banks simply aren't issuing businesses the point-of-sale terminals that are required for credit card acceptance unless the operator of the business comes up with a huge deposit, and most small restaurant owners don't have the resources.

The second reason many businesses in Chinatown don't take credit cards is, of course, tax. If you do a lot of cash business, you can avoid paying tax by understating your revenues. If there's no record of what you took in, it's pretty simple to steal from the business and the taxman, too. I should also mention that there is a significant cultural factor here as well. Historically, tax investigators were unable to make cases in the various ethnic communities because of those communities' inherent distrust of the authorities, combined with a complete lack of the necessary language skills on the part of the authorities. However, this is changing, since most of the Chinese and other Asian communities have grown large enough and have been in North America long enough that their children have become tax investigators and police officers.

And, of course, there is always the possibility that someone is using the business to launder money.

Ya Gotta Leave Your Keys

Here's another example of a cash business. Let's suppose you operate a basic one-level parking lot in the downtown core of a major North American city. You have 80 spaces, and parking for the business day costs $15; ideally, with all spaces full for the business day, you will generate $1,200 per day. On 250 business days per year, you should generate $300,000. But the lot is also open at night, there are lots of sporting events, there are no "in and out" privileges, and people park on weekends when they're shopping—and so on and so on.

So you could probably declare around $300,000 to $400,000 per year and the taxman would leave you alone. But what if you start spending a few weekends each year smuggling illegal immigrants, and netting another $350,000 doing that? It's a pretty easy thing to inject those proceeds into the bank deposit from the parking lot. The taxman doesn't care how you make your money, just as long as you pay tax on it.

Admittedly, this example is a pretty simple one. But if you're a bank manager and your parking lot client starts increasing his deposits (a) will you even notice it? And (b) will you have the nerve to confront him about it? After all, he's a nice guy, isn't he? Hey, isn't he the same guy who lets you park for free?

You Want Fries with That?

If honest business people find themselves in competition with money launderers, they may never know what hit them.

Peter, Paul and Mary are friends, and their dream has always been to go into the restaurant business together. They scrimp and save for years and finally get their start. They buy a small place in the theater district. In order to do this, all three of them went to the bank. They mortgaged everything, gave personal guarantees…and if this place doesn't make it, they're screwed.

But it does make it. After a couple of years, things are going pretty well; the place has a good reputation and is becoming fashionable. Because of its proximity to the theaters, before- and after-show business is booming. Peter, Paul and Mary are finally making money. Not very much money, because the margins are small and they all still have substantial mortgages on their homes. But they're making it. One of the reasons is their chef. He's a charismatic guy, popular with the customers and very visible in the restaurant. They pay him a huge salary, but he's worth it because his name is known and he gets them lots of publicity. If you want a table, you need a reservation. It's very busy, and so, as is usually the case, other restaurants start to spring up around Peter, Paul and Mary's to handle the overflow. PP&M don't mind. They're nice people and competition is a good thing.

There's a place right across the street that is doing OK. Not great, just OK. They know it's up for sale, but it's a very old place and the building improvements that would be required are prohibitive.

Enter Vinnie the coke dealer. Although decidedly lacking in formal education, Vinnie is an entrepreneur. He understands the concept of a free market economy, although he probably can't spell it. He generates about $50,000 per week from his cocaine trafficking organization and he's swimming in cash. For years, he has been using these two Cuban guys to clean up his cash, but recently they told him that the cost of their service is going up. From now on, the Cubans will take twenty cents of every dollar they move for him. Vinnie comes up with a brand-new plan. Why not buy a restaurant?

He buys the restaurant across the street from PP&M's place for $150,000. For weeks, contractors feverishly renovate Vinnie's. PP&M can't believe that anyone would spend that much money on a place like that. But Vinnie does, and eventually he opens.

After a few weeks, PP&M notice that Vinnie's is having a happy hour promotion, selling drinks at half price. It's a great idea, but there's no way that they could afford to do it. They can't figure out how Vinnie is managing it either, profits being what they are in the restaurant business.

The following month, Vinnie runs a steak and lobster special for $8.95 per person. PP&M buy their steak from the same supplier as Vinnie, and they know that the wholesale price of the steak alone is almost $10. How can Vinnie sell it, with lobster, for $8.95?

The chef comes to see PP&M. He announces that he will be leaving to take another position at another restaurant where there is an opportunity to make more money and not be so constrained by costs. That's right—Vinnie's.

Within a week, three of their best waiters and their wine guy have also gone across the street. PP&M's restaurant is suddenly in trouble. Vinnie's now has all the top staff, all the best entertainment and the greatest food in the city. Eventually, PP&M's can't compete. The restaurant closes. They are forced to declare bankruptcy. All three of them default on their mortgages and lose their homes.

Benny the Banker, who gave PP&M the loan, and whose wife is eight months pregnant, discovers that the repossessed homes won't cover the note and he has to report to his bosses at the bank that they are facing a substantial bad debt. Meanwhile, Vinnie is getting bored. He gets bored easily, and running a restaurant isn't all it's cracked up to be. He decides to sell the place.

Along comes Elton. Elton is long on cash and short on experience but is interested in creating a fine dining establishment that caters exclusively to the city's gay community. He takes a look at Vinnie's financial statements (unaudited, of course) and decides to go for it. He goes to see Benny the Banker and takes out a loan to purchase the restaurant from Vinnie. The selling price is $1 million.

Vinnie is happy to be rid of the place. Benny the Banker, trying to redeem himself with his bosses, is happy to report that he has just written a loan for $800,000 to Elton.

After a few weeks, Elton is worried. He can't figure out what he's doing wrong; he hasn't really changed anything, yet it seems like the money is just flying out the door and there's no profit. It seems to Elton that Vinnie was buying $10 worth of steak and selling it for $9, but that wouldn't make sense, would it?

Within two months, the money runs out and Elton has to close his place. He defaults on his loan and loses the condo he put up as collateral. Benny the Banker, who now has a new baby at home, has to admit to his bosses that he's stuck them with one more non-performing restaurant loan.

Of course, Vinnie was losing money on the restaurant, too, but he didn't care, because he set up the business to launder his cocaine profits. He had no problem with a consistent 10 percent loss. It was cheaper than the 20 percent he would have had to pay the Cubans.

Vinnie had plenty of drug cash to inject into his business, so it appeared to be making money when it really wasn't. When he sold the restaurant, which he had originally purchased for $150,000, he made a "legitimate" profit of $850,000 because he had artificially raised the value of the restaurant with his drug money.

So what ends up happening?

Vinnie makes a better deal with the Cubans and decides to stick to the drug business.

Peter ends up as the french fry captain at a Burger King.

Paul runs away and gets a job herding donairs on a Lebanese ranch.

Mary and the chef find work selling kitchen gadgets on the Home Shopping Channel, where they become famous for coining the phrase, "Set it and forget it!"

Elton quits the restaurant business for good, shaves his legs and joins the off-Broadway production of *Stomp!*

Benny the Banker is forced to get a job as the change boy at a porno parlor, subsequently acquiring the new nickname of "Benny the Wanker."

But money laundering doesn't really hurt anybody does it? I mean, it's just money, right? it's not like you're murdering people or anything, is it?

Swingers

Sometimes legitimate business operators can become unwilling partners in a money laundering operation just by doing a cash transaction. Million-dollar cash deals are kind of unusual, but here's an example.

Skip is the president of a very old, established and profitable company located in the Detroit area. The company was started by his grandfather and manufactures fluorescent tubes and light bulbs for the North American market. The company is privately held and has no debt at all. Needless to say, Skip isn't hurting for money.

Two years ago, at his golf club, Skip met Hector, a Panamanian businessman who relocated to the United States during the Noriega years. Hector has a very successful import/export business and is involved in the exportation of consumer products, particularly dry goods, to Latin America.

One day, during a round of golf, Hector approaches Skip with a proposition. Hector says that he has a buyer in Venezuela who is interested in purchasing $1 million dollars worth of fluorescent tubes. Skip tells Hector that his company currently has excessive amounts of inventory in their warehouse and they could deliver that amount immediately. They agree to do the deal.

Shortly before they close the deal, Hector tells Skip that there's one small problem. Because of some foreign exchange issues that are too complex to explain, Hector must make payment for the fluorescent tubes in cash. He apologizes profusely and tells Skip that he is willing to pay him a slightly higher price per tube for the inconvenience. Skip thinks it over and decides that, although the cash is a problem, he can do it. The company's cash flow is strong and he's quite sure that he can pocket the cash without ever having it touch the books. Besides, he has several million dollars in fluorescent tubes gathering dust in the warehouse.

What Skip doesn't know is that Hector is part of a sophisticated money laundering organization. Skip doesn't even consider it because Hector and his wife are such nice people and he's known them a long time. Besides, Colombian money launderers don't play golf and, even if they did, they couldn't get accepted for a membership at his course. To top it off, Skip and his wife just had a new home built and it came with a floor safe. This is going to be his first opportunity to use it!

Everything goes without a hitch. In the clubhouse, just prior to teeing off one Saturday morning, Hector asks Skip for his car keys. When Skip puts his clubs in the trunk after the golf game, there is a gym bag with $1 million dollars in the trunk of his car. He rushes home and puts it in the new floor safe.

Hector takes delivery of the fluorescent tubes and loads them into half a dozen forty-foot "cans"[*] and ships them to Colombia. When they arrive in Colombia, Hector's people bribe the customs inspectors to allow the shipment to pass through the port without any duty and taxes being paid. The tubes are distributed throughout Colombia and Venezuela on the gray market. If you travel to Bogotá, you will see people on almost every street corner, selling things. Everything from Marlboros to TV sets, still in the case. Lately, there are guys selling fluorescent tubes as well.

[*] Sea containers.

Meanwhile, back up north, Skip slowly begins to walk off a million dollars in cash. Instead of using his credit cards, he pays cash for everything that he can. Before too long, he's starting to make a small dent in it.

Skip's wife wants to put in a pool. They have a meeting with the contractor that built their home and look at the plans. This is some pool! With all the extras that his wife wants, like a sauna and a shower and a bar and a kitchen, the contractor tells Skip that he can do it for $350,000. As they are standing in the driveway, he tells Skip that if he wants to do a cash deal, he'll do it for $300,000. Skip agrees.

The pool is installed, the contractor gets his cash, and no one is the wiser. The contractor pays most of his sub-trades in cash: the concrete guy, the electrician, the plumber, his cousin who installed the barbecue. They are small contractors and they'd all rather not pay tax if they can avoid it.

Now meet Juan-Fernando. Juan-Fernando is the Colombian equivalent of Skip. Older, established family; many years in the fluorescent tube manufacturing business. The difference is, Juan-Fernando's company is not doing all that well. It seems that recently, the Columbian market has been flooded with cheap fluorescent tubes. These tubes are being sold for less money than it takes for Juan-Fernando to make them.

This whole scenario is a one-time deal for Skip. It will be his only direct, albeit unwitting, interaction with organized crime. He will go back to his life and that will be the end of it. After all, no one got hurt by Skip's actions, did they?

The pool contractor and his sub-tradesmen are happy. They got paid, and in cash, too! They didn't have to pay any tax. Who's that going to hurt? The tax people take enough of their money anyway, don't they?

Hector has successfully circumvented the Colombian exchange

controls by generating Colombian pesos on the sale of the fluorescent tubes. He has also contributed to the continuing cycle of corruption of Colombian government officials by bribing the customs inspectors.

Juan-Fernando eventually has to close his company in Colombia. Times were already tough and that last flurry of cheap tubes on the black market did him in. All of his employees lose their jobs. There is no work for them in Bogotá and they are forced to return to the small villages from whence they came. To feed their families, Juan-Fernando's employees get jobs picking coca leaves.

But that's not Skip's fault, is it?

...

Conclusion

If you're involved in business, and maybe even if you aren't, there's a pretty good chance you may encounter money that is the proceeds of criminal activity. If you suspect that it is, the responsibility is yours, as a citizen, to try and do something about it.

Although under the law you will likely only be found guilty if it can be proven that you knew the money in question was the proceeds of crime, your involvement, even unwittingly, in a money laundering scheme could still ruin your reputation. If the story gets out, it won't matter that you weren't convicted of any crime. Here's how the press will report it and how the public will perceive it:

- They will say that you were involved in drug trafficking.
- They will say that you were involved in money laundering.
- They know that terrorists and organized crime traffic drugs and launder money.
- They know that terrorists and organized crime cause the deaths of innocent people.
- They will say that you helped them.

And when they say that, they'll be right.

ENDNOTES

1. United States Bureau of Engraving and Printing, $2 Note Fact Sheet
2. Interview with Mr. Ian Dear, Vice-President, Bank of America, May 15, 2003
3. *Insurance Day*, June 13, 2003, "Art for money's sake"
4. *New York Times*, December 3, 1993, "Head of Medellin cocaine cartel is killed by troops in Colombia," by Robert D. McFadden
5. Agence France Presse, September 12, 1996, "Police may have confiscated late drug lord's Picasso painting"
6. *Los Angeles Times*, November 2, 2000, "Softening the face of Medellin," by Juanita Darling
7. EFE News Service, February 12, 2003, "Government seizes riches of Colombian drug lord"
8. Department of State Bulletin, November 1989, Vol. 89, No. 2152, "The OAS and the Panama Crisis; Organization of American States, Lawrence S. Eagleburger statement; transcript[7]"
9. Ibid.
10. Ibid.
11. *New York Times*, July 25, 1999, "Russian gangsters exploit capitalism to increase profits," by Raymond Bonner
12. YBM press conference remarks, Patrick L. Meehan, U.S. Attorney for the Eastern District of Pennsylvania, April 24, 2003
13. *Toronto Star*, December 1, 2002, "Magnets and the mob. YBM

debacle a key test for OSC," by Madhavi Acharya and Tom Yew

14. *United States* v. *Semion Mogilevich et al.*, Criminal No. 02-157, United States District Court for the Eastern District of Pennsylvania

15. *United States* v. *Berlin et al.*, Case No. S1-99-CR-914 (SWK) (SDNY)

16. *USA Today*, September 23, 1999, "Bank chief says workers used poor judgment," by Thomas A. Fogarty

17. *Corporate Counsel*, April 1, 2001, "Sins of the U.S. bankers," by John Anderson

18. *USA Today*, September 23, 1999, "Bank chief says workers used poor judgment," by Thomas A. Fogarty

19. *New York Times*, July 25, 1999, "Russian gangsters exploit capitalism to increase profits," by Raymond Bonner

20. *Moscow Times*, September 3, 1998, "Swiss embassy worried by Mafia trial," by Simon Saradzhyan

21. *Washington Times*, August 30, 1999, "Who wasn't minding the bear?" by Arnaud de Borchgrave

22. Statement of Mr. Steven W. Casteel, Assistant Administrator for Intelligence, Drug Enforcement Administration, Federal Document Clearing House Congressional Testimony; Capitol Hill Hearing Testimony, Senate Judiciary Committee, May 20, 2003

23. Federal Document Clearing House, House International Relations Committee, "U.S. Representative Henry Hyde (R-Il) Holds Hearing On International Global Terrorism: Its Links With Illicit Drugs As Illustrated By The IRA And Other Groups In Colombia," Washington, D.C., April 24, 2002

24. *Anannova (Orange) News*, November 29, 2002, www.anannova. com

25. *South Florida Business Journal*, October 26, 2001, "FIU study: Honey trade launders al Qaeda cash," by Jim Freer

26. Presentation by Mr. Ian Huntington to the South African Law Reform Commission conference on money laundering, "Money Laundering: The Road Ahead," Johannesburg, Republic of South Africa, 1996

27. Testimony of Robert M. Morgenthau, Manhattan District Attorney, New York, New York, United States Senate Governmental Affairs Committee, Permanent Subcommittee on Investigations, July 18, 2001

28. U.S. Department of State, International Information Programs news release dated November 27, 2001: "U.S., U.K. Sign Cayman Islands Tax Information Exchange Pact"

29. United States Customs Service, June 1999, "Black Market Peso Exchange: A Trade Based Money Laundering System"

30. Testimony of Ambassador Stuart E. Eizenstat, U.S. House of Representatives Financial Services Committee, Washington, D.C., October 3, 2001

31. *CIA World Factbook*, 2002

32. Financial Action Task Force, Annual Review of Non-Cooperative Countries or Territories, June 20, 2003

33. *Corporate Counsel*, April 1, 2001, "Sins of the U.S. bankers," by John Anderson

34. Agence France Presse, August 22, 2001, "Former prosecutor fingers top Russian politicians for money laundering"

35. *Washington Times*, August 30, 1999, "Who wasn't minding the bear?" by Arnaud de Borchgrave

36. *What The Papers Say (Russia)*, March 3, 2003, "Stolen billions" by Oleg Lurie, translated by Arina Yevtikhova

37. *Washington Times*, August 30, 1999, "Who wasn't minding the bear?" by Arnaud de Borchgrave

38. Money Laundering Alert, April 2001, "Senate panel presses large U.S. banks on abuses, airs new findings"

39. *Christian Science Monitor*, December 26, 2002, "Blowing

Smoke: The complexity of the drug war in a single murder," by Roger Gathman. Review of *Down by the River: Drugs, Money, Murder and Family*, by Charles Bowden, 2002

40. *The Guardian*, June 14, 2001, "Mexico and U.S. claim success in war on drugs," by Duncan Campbell and Jo Tuckman.

41. Money Laundering Alert, September 1998, "Mexican bank controlled by cartel said to move millions in U.S."

42. United States Federal Court, Case No. 98-Civ-2517, S. Dis. Fla, Affidavit of Special Agent Vincent Lozowicki, Internal Revenue Service, Criminal Investigation Division, dated April 1998, Case No. 98-Civ-2517, S. Dis. Fla

43. *Los Angeles Times*, May 9, 1999, "Hand-over of laundered $3 million sets precedent in drug wars," by Mark Fineman

44. *National Post*, July 14, 2003, Editorial, "Canada's pampered Criminals"

45. *Los Angeles Times*, April 1, 1992, "Two deputies called part of conspiracy of corrupt officers," by Victor Merina

46. *Frontline*, October 16, 1990, "Drug Wars," produced by Charles Stuart and Marcia Vivancos

INDEX